INTRODUCTION
TO THE LOTUS SUTRA

INTRODUCTION
TO THE
LOTUS
SUTRA

by Yoshiro Tamura

EDITED AND INTRODUCED BY
Gene Reeves

TRANSLATED BY
Gene Reeves
and Michio Shinozaki

WISDOM PUBLICATIONS · BOSTON

Wisdom Publications
199 Elm Street
Somerville, MA 02144 USA
www.wisdompubs.org

Library of Congress Cataloging-in-Publication Data
Tamura, Yoshiro, 1921–1989, author.
  [Hokekkyo. English]
  Introduction to the Lotus Sutra / by Yoshiro Tamura ; edited and introduced by Gene Reeves ; translated by Gene Reeves and Michio Shinozaki.
    pages cm
  Includes bibliographical references and index.
  Includes translation from Japanese.
  ISBN 1-61429-080-6 (pbk. : alk. paper)
  1. Tripitaka. Sutrapitaka. Saddharmapundarikasutra—Criticism, interpretation, etc. I. Reeves, Gene, editor, translator. II. Shinozaki, Michio, translator. III. Title.
  BQ2057.T3513 2014
  294.3'85—dc23

                        2014000057

ISBN 978-1-61429-080-3   Ebook ISBN 978-1-61429-099-5

18 17 16 15 14
5 4 3 2 1

Cover painting by Shi Ya courtesy of Inkdance Chinese Painting Gallery, www.inkdancechinesepaintings.com.
Cover design by TL. Interior design by Gopa&Ted2, Inc. Set in Adobe Garamond Premier Pro 11/14.7. The photograph of Yoshiro Tamura on page 194 is courtesy of Kosei Publishing.

Wisdom Publications' books are printed on acid-free paper and meet the guidelines for permanence and durability of the Production Guidelines for Book Longevity of the Council on Library Resources.

This book was produced with environmental mindfulness. We have elected to print this title on 30% PCW recycled paper. As a result, we have saved the following resources: 8 trees, 4 million BTUs of energy, 726 lbs. of greenhouse gases, 3,938 gallons of water, and 264 lbs. of solid waste. For more information, please visit our website, www.wisdompubs.org.

Printed in the United States of America.

Contents

Publisher's Acknowledgment

THE PUBLISHER gratefully acknowledges the generous contribution of the Hershey Family Foundation toward the publication of this book.

Introduction to the Lotus Sutra

Introduction

O N A VISIT to Japan in the autumn of 1983, I had the good fortune of being introduced to Yoshiro Tamura (1921–89) through arrangements made by Nikkyo Niwano, the founder and then president of Rissho Kosei-kai. Soon we were able to arrange for Prof. Tamura to come to Chicago the following spring to give a series of lectures on the Lotus Sutra at Meadville Lombard Theological School at the University of Chicago. Since those lectures were very well received, Tamura was invited back to the University of Chicago as Numata Professor in the spring of 1985. During subsequent years I met Tamura many times, both in Chicago and in Japan. He was a key member in a series of small conferences that I had organized in Chicago and in Japan. It was partly on account of Tamura's encouragement that my own interest in the Lotus Sutra grew enormously during that time. Together, Tamura and I cooked up a few projects related to the Lotus Sutra, which led to my eventual move to Japan in January of 1989, in part to work with and to continue to learn from him.

Unfortunately, our collaboration was not to be realized. Just before I left Chicago to go to Japan, Tamura was diagnosed with liver cancer. He passed away less than three months later. It was shortly after this that Michio Shinozaki, then Dean of Rissho Kosei-kai's Gakurin Seminary, and I committed ourselves to translating Tamura's small introduction to the Lotus Sutra, *The Lotus Sutra: Truth • Life • Practice.*[1]

Tamura was not a popular writer. When we met he was a professor at Rissho University, Nichiren-shu's university in Tokyo. This followed his retirement from the University of Tokyo in 1982, where he held the chair in Japanese Buddhism. He was an academic and a historian. Yet he also had a kind of layman's love of the Lotus Sutra, which is reflected in his preface to this book. He knew as well as anyone that the Lotus Sutra was not merely something fit for academic scrutiny, but a religious text very much alive in the contemporary world.

His small book, first published in Japan in 1969, was intended for a popular audience. It introduces the teachings of the Lotus Sutra, some of the scholarly work on its composition, and the role it has had in East Asian, especially Japanese, history. Part of a popular but sophisticated series, the book was intended to inform educated, nonspecialist Japanese readers about the Lotus Sutra and its uses and evaluations in history. Since the Lotus Sutra is the primary Buddhist text for several traditional Japanese Buddhist denominations of the Nichiren and Tendai traditions, as well as for several new Buddhist organizations that emerged in the twentieth century, particularly for the Reiyukai, Rissho Kosei-kai, and Soka Gakkai, the number of potential readers in contemporary Japan would have been very substantial. Well over twenty million Japanese recite regularly from the Lotus Sutra.

So the audience Tamura intended for his book was not made up of his fellow academics—at least not primarily—but of serious lay Buddhists who already had some familiarity with the Lotus Sutra. Of course, we cannot assume as much familiarity with the Lotus Sutra on the part of an English reading audience. But with the growing popularity of many varieties of Buddhism in the United States and Europe, the number of people in those lands that know of the Lotus Sutra can be presumed to be growing, too. We hope that this revision and translation of Tamura's introduction to the Lotus Sutra will deepen for many their understanding of the Sutra, and broaden their understanding and appreciation of Buddhism in general by historically situating the Sutra and surveying its contributions to the development of East Asian Buddhist thought.

Tamura was raised in a Christian family, but he soon grew dissatisfied with Christianity for a variety of reasons and did not maintain any affiliation with the church as an adult. While it would be fair, I think, to say that he was deeply impressed by teachings of the Lotus Sutra and enjoyed friendly relations with several Buddhist organizations, including the traditional Nichiren-shu and the modern Rissho Kosei-kai, so far as I know, he never became a practicing member of any religious organization. Like many of his academic colleagues, Tamura was religiously unaffiliated.

In Japan and among students of Japanese Buddhism, Tamura is most famous for his controversial appraisal of Tendai thought, particularly of "original enlightenment thought."[2] In this introduction too, Tamura claimed that Buddhist philosophy reached its zenith with Tendai original enlightenment thought. He was, in fact, an advocate of this way of thinking, not only as a way of thinking within Buddhism, but as a positive influence on Japanese thought and culture. In more recent years, this aspect of Tendai thought has received a good bit of criticism, primarily for fostering an uncritical attitude toward the status quo, and thereby sanctioning discrimination and injustice. Noriaki Hakamaya, whose critical Buddhism is aimed more squarely at the Kyoto school of Nishida and Nishitani than at Tamura, finds in original enlightenment thought an instance of what he calls "topical Buddhism": a Buddhism that embraces a kind of monistic, absolute, unchanging, substantial ground of all things. Hakamaya finds such views more akin to Hinduism or Taoism than to "authentic" Buddhism, or to what one finds in the Lotus Sutra.[3]

Some might think that the section of this book dealing with Tendai thought should be updated somehow to reflect how Tamura would have responded to recent critiques of Tendai original enlightenment thought. In fact, we can only speculate on how Tamura might have responded to such developments. My own guess is that he would have rejected any form of monistic ground, while supporting the affirmation of the reality of all things, a notion found both in the Lotus Sutra and some forms of Tendai original enlightenment thought. But, since this is simply speculation on my part, it would seem inappropriate to change Tamura's text to reflect developments of which he was not a part.[4]

Though Tamura does discuss Tendai thought in this book, it is really about the Lotus Sutra, and very little of what is known about the Lotus Sutra has changed since Tamura wrote it. There are a variety of opinions on certain matters related to the history of the Sutra, such as why the Sanskrit originals of the Lotus from which Chinese translations were made have never been found, some of which differ from Tamura's view. But this would be true even if Tamura were writing the book today.

This translation does revise Tamura's text in some ways. In a few places, relatively minor things have been brought up to date, and a few of the more obscure references have been omitted. The biggest change is the omission of substantial biographical sections from the latter part of the text. Tamura had included there several brief biographies of Japanese men who were prominent followers of the Lotus Sutra in the late nineteenth and early twentieth centuries. Almost none of these figures are well known outside of Japan.[5] I hope to include the excised biographies in another work that will be a collection of biographies of Chinese and Japanese men and women whose lives were greatly impacted by the Lotus Sutra. Tamura's intent in this part of the book was obviously to show the variety of ways in which devotion to the Lotus Sutra had been put into practice, that is, how it had been embodied in social and political life.

Introduction to the Lotus Sutra is, I believe, a superb introduction to the Sutra. While it is not a substitute for delving deeply into the Sutra itself, or for studying other scholarly and nonscholarly views of it, it is a fine introduction to the work. Tamura introduces the main teachings found in the Lotus Sutra, the generally accepted scholarly account of how the Sutra was compiled in stages, an outline of traditional interpretations of it, and a survey of its importance and influence in Japanese life and culture. One could, of course, ask for more in any of these areas, but supplying more details, more extensive discussion, and greater treatment of contemporary scholarly views would call for a different kind of book. This book serves as a wonderful introduction to the Lotus Sutra and its place in history, and will be of value to people interested in the Sutra for religious reasons and for students interested in enriching their understanding of Mahayana Buddhism.

Gene Reeves

Tamura's Preface

S OON AFTER ENTERING university in December of 1943, I was sent to the front as a student soldier. I wondered if I were allowed to bring but a single book on the trip, possibly to my death, which would I want to bring? Many of my fellow student soldiers were thinking the same thing. We all worked at part-time jobs in order to be able to buy books, and we often lent them to each other. Yet we were perplexed by the idea of selecting only one. One fellow insisted on bringing Kant's *Critique of Pure Reason.* Some Christian students, not surprisingly, chose the Bible, as was natural for Christians.

Since in those days my own interest was shifting from Western philosophy to Buddhist thought, I decided to select one appropriate book from among the many related to Buddhism. It was the Lotus Sutra.

The Lotus Sutra—the so-called Buddhist Bible—has long been read by people of many different Buddhist sects. It has so influenced the literature and thought of Japan that a new genre of "Lotus literature" was created. It has also spread among common people, providing spiritual support in their daily lives. In modern times, several thinkers and literary people have appeared who based their lives on the Lotus Sutra.

When the Lotus Sutra was translated and introduced to China, it was called the teaching that unifies all ideas.[6] Zhiyi (538–597)[7] later attempted to establish a unified Buddhism based on the Lotus Sutra, just as the Sui dynasty was attempting to unify all of China. By establishing a unified Buddhism, Zhiyi sought to provide a comprehensive and unified worldview and philosophy of life based on Buddhism. The Lotus Sutra was seen as an excellent systematic theory to that end. The rediscovery of the truly profound thought contained in the narrative and literary expression of the Lotus Sutra brought forth, in a sense, the so-called Tiantai[8] Lotus philosophy.

Tiantai Lotus philosophy came from China to Japan along with the Lotus Sutra, and was further transformed by new developments there. Dengyo Daishi, Saicho, founded the Japanese Tendai school at Mt. Hiei. Mt. Hiei was later to become a temple of truth and played a central role not only within Japanese Buddhism but with respect to intellectual thought in Japan in general as well. There, under the influence of the Lotus Sutra, various typically Buddhist ideas were collected, edited, and sometimes intensified, and Buddhist philosophy reached its highest level, known as "Tendai original enlightenment thought." This was a "breakthrough," going beyond the limitations of ordinary human thinking. As a result it evolved into an exposition of a monistic worldview. We could say that it carried Buddhist thought to an extreme. This original enlightenment thought has been influential not only on Japanese Buddhism, but also on various branches of Japanese art and culture.

The founders of the new Buddhism of Kamakura—Honen, Shinran, Dogen, Nichiren and others—had all once been student monks at Mt. Hiei, just outside of Kyoto, and had learned Tendai Lotus or Tendai original enlightenment thought there. Among them, Dogen and Nichiren retained a close relationship with the Lotus Sutra to the end. In Dogen's great work, *Treasury of the True Dharma-Eye*,[9] among citations from many sutras, those from the Lotus Sutra are most frequent, and we can also identify additional passages that seem to teach Lotus philosophical theory. In this sense, it can be said that one cannot understand the *Treasury of the True Dharma-Eye* without knowing the Lotus Sutra. And, as the story goes, when Dogen himself realized that he had a serious illness, he prepared himself for death by reciting passages from the Lotus Sutra.

Nichiren also devoted himself to the Lotus Sutra and relied on Tendai Lotus theory in his everyday life. Yet, suffering from several persecutions during his life, such as being exiled, he gradually changed his perspective toward the Lotus Sutra. The sutra consists of three major parts: the first elucidates a unifying truth of the universe (the Wonderful Dharma of One Vehicle); the second sheds light on everlasting personal life (the Everlasting Original Buddha); and the third emphasizes the actual activities of human beings (the bodhisattva way). In brief, there are three major kinds of teaching in the Lotus Sutra, which correspond to truth, life, and practice. Nichiren shifted the focus of his attention to the third.

In this third part, emphasis is placed on the practice of devoting one's life completely to the sutra, and those who practice it are praised and presented as apostles of the Buddha, dispatched by him to this world with the mission of embodying the Buddha's truth in this world. Though grief stricken by hardship, by reading this part with his whole heart and mind, Nichiren was inspired, gained courage to live and be joyous, was enabled to accept suffering with a self-respecting, even elitist, consciousness of being the Buddha's disciple, and could fight against the secular authorities. He also grew eager to reform the world socially and to establish an ideal state of world peace. This idea has been passed down to followers of Nichiren who are devoted to the Lotus Sutra, giving rise to powerful Nichiren movements in modern and recent times.

The Lotus Sutra, however, is also a mysterious sutra. This is because on the one hand, it has been highly revered, and on the other, it has had the opposite reputation. During the Tokugawa period a variety of theories critical of Buddhism arose, and others that were outright anti-Buddhist. One was the theory that the content of the Lotus Sutra is vacuous. Atsutane Hirata and others criticized the Lotus Sutra as being empty puffery, nothing more than snake oil medicine. Hirata's snake oil theory subsequently grew in fame and is still known today. Some modern Buddhist scholars, as well, criticize the Lotus Sutra for having no theory and for emphasizing martyrdom, saying that by giving an exclusive and closed impression it has created a group that is estranged from mainstream society. Thus there is the strange situation in which the Lotus Sutra has reputations at opposite extremes. As I will discuss some of the seven wonders of Buddhism at the beginning of this book, we can count this matter of having reputations at opposite extremes as one of those wonders.

Leaving ten soldiers behind, my military unit was moved to the Philippines and suffered a crushing defeat just before landing there. I was one of the ten who remained behind. As he was leaving, the commander of my company asked me to teach him a few passages from a sutra that would be suitable for mourning the dead. I gave him some famous verses taken from chapter 16 of the Lotus Sutra, "The Lifetime of the Tathagata." I imagine that that company commander died with his soldiers before he had time to mourn them. Later, I was ordered to transfer several times, and I sometimes had to face death. But I was never without the Lotus Sutra. When I was discharged, my copy of the sutra was more worn out than I was.

I am filled with deep emotion as I set out to explain the Lotus Sutra, the book that has been the most important in my own life.

End of June 1969
Yoshiro Tamura

I

Formation of the Lotus Sutra

I

Are Sutras the Words of the Buddha?

Some of the Wonders of Buddhism

THE LOTUS SUTRA in Sanskrit, like many other sutras, begins with the words *evam maya shrutam*—"This is what I heard." The "I" indicates Ananda, one of the ten great disciples of the Buddha, for many years Shakyamuni's personal attendant. He was first among the disciples in memorizing Shakyamuni's sermons, and so he was called "first and foremost in hearing the sermons." At the meeting for compiling the sutras after the Buddha's death, Ananda recited the teachings he had memorized, beginning with the words "This is what I heard." That is why, they say, the words *evam maya shrutam* were added at the beginning of the sutras. It is also said that when Shakyamuni passed away, he ordered Ananda to add such a phrase at the beginning in order to distinguish Buddhist sutras from sutras of other faiths. But this is no more than a legend.

In some sutras, the "I" need not be identified with Ananda. But the Buddhist sutras are supposed to have been told as Ananda or other disciples heard them from Shakyamuni. In other words, the sutras are supposed to have been faithful records of the teachings and words of Shakyamuni Buddha, and so they have been revered from ancient times as the "golden mouth" or "direct sermons" of Shakyamuni. It is a wonder, however, that there is such an extremely vast number of sutras that are direct sermons of Shakyamuni.

Collectively, the sutras are called the "Great Collection of Sutras." This is the so-called tripitaka or "three baskets," the three divisions of the Buddhist scriptures: the Buddha's teaching (*sutra*); the precepts and rules of the community of monks and nuns (*vinaya*); and commentaries on the Buddha's teachings (*abhidharma*). A strict interpretation of the meaning of "sutra" should exclude vinaya and abhidharma from the Buddha's teachings, the sutras. But the sutras, even when taken alone, constitute a great number of volumes. From ancient times, Chinese and Tibetan versions were translated, and Sanskrit and Pali texts were composed, thus producing a variety of lists and catalogs. If we count only sutras as such, excluding those that are only duplicates, the total number of sutras is over six thousand.

In Christianity there is only one Bible. A single sutra is often equivalent to several books of the Bible. Why were so many Buddhist sutras produced? This is one of the wonders of Buddhism. Modern readers, having a more critical stance toward the tradition, easily surmised that most sutras were produced over a long period of time following the death of Shakyamuni. If we read a sutra and see that it is full of fantasy and fiction, and the Lotus Sutra is no exception, we know that it is the product of a later period and could not be the direct words of Shakyamuni Buddha.

Since we can readily see that later Buddhists freely produced sutras, why was it claimed, by labeling them "sutras," that they were the word of Shakyamuni? We might find such use of the Buddha's name very audacious. It is, in fact, audacious. There are several reasons for it. One is that Indians were not very interested in history. It is generally said that India does not have histories. Setting aside the question of whether this is actually true, it is the case, generally speaking, that Indians were more interested in the boundless and unlimited that goes beyond this concrete, historical world.

Study of and devotion to the Lotus Sutra have been popular since it appeared in India, China, and Japan, but the interest in it is quite different in each case. In India interest in it was particularly characterized by the universality and equality of truth. We can see the Indian way of thinking in such transhistorical interests. Thus, Indian Buddhists were relatively uninterested in historical facts about Shakyamuni, and so they asserted without hesitation that later sutras were the words of Shakyamuni. This is not the only reason, but it does allow us to understand to some extent the phenomenon of attributing later sutras to Shakyamuni.

After the sutras were introduced into China and translated into Chinese, many Chinese translations were preserved. But the texts from which they were translated have completely disappeared, and we do not know what happened to them. At the present time we only have original Sanskrit texts—or to be more precise, copies of Sanskrit texts—discovered in Nepal, Central Asia, and other places, from the nineteenth century on.

The disappearance of the Sanskrit texts in China may have been due to such things as long periods of war or frequent anti-Buddhist movements. But even during those times, Chinese Buddhists contrived numerous ways of preserving Chinese sutras. Moving them to Korea or Japan was one; carving sutras into stone was another. When movements to revive Buddhism arose, the scattered Chinese sutras and commentaries had to be searched for in many places, even by dispatching people to Korea or Japan for that purpose. Yet we find no evidence of such an effort as far as the original texts are concerned. There were instances of people going to India to find additional original texts and successfully bringing them back to China after great hardship. But even these texts vanished once they had been translated. In any event, sooner or later they disappeared.

Other reasons must also be sought. One lies in the Sino-centrism of the Chinese. It was a matter of pride for the Chinese that China is called the center of the world—the Middle Kingdom.[10] Under the influence of this kind of thinking, translated sutras gained authority, and once they were translated the original texts were probably discarded without a second thought.

There are probably other reasons as well. The Chinese, for example, are said to be a people who value a pragmatic, down-to-earth way of life. When Chinese wisdom, which is thought to consist of statesmanship and the art of living, is applied to sutras, sutras written in Chinese are deemed nearer to a practical way of life and more useful for the Chinese. Thus the texts that were chiefly used in China were in Chinese, and the texts from which they were translated became more and more distant.

These reasons for the disappearance of the Indian texts in China are little more than speculation. We have to await further research. In Japan, sutras inherited from China have been used as they are and have never really been translated into Japanese. No wonder we call this another wonder! If we contrast the Chinese use of Indian texts with the Japanese use of Chinese texts in order to probe the reasons for both, we may discover a first step to understanding both of these wonders.

As we reflected on the Buddhist history of the three countries, we glimpsed various wonders, which we can count among the seven wonders of Buddhism. Although Buddhism is not supposed to be polytheistic, all sorts of buddhas have been recognized and worshipped. So much so that ordinary people may feel mystified by this. Even now, within a single sect we see different examples of the main object of worship from temple to temple.

Those within the Buddhist fold fear offending its authorities if they raise questions or point out its wonders, and they worry about drawing attention to themselves or having the purity of their faith questioned by their own sect. But ordinary people will readily notice that there are a number of such wonders within Buddhism.

Mahayana Buddhism Is Not the Words of the Buddha

European and modern scientific research methods were introduced into Japan, and into the field of Buddhist studies during the Meiji period, and Japanese scholars undertook to study original texts and do historical research on them. Along with this came the theory that the Mahayana is not the words of the Buddha—that is to say, the idea that Mahayana sutras are not authentic sermons of Shakyamuni. There was a call for a return to an early, or fundamental, form of Buddhism.

Most distinguished Japanese scholars of Buddhism devoted themselves to the study of early Buddhism. Masaharu Anesaki (1873–1949),[11] who founded the Department of Religious Studies at the University of Tokyo, said in the preface to his *Historical Buddha and Dharmakaya Buddha*[12] that the eternal truth is to be seen in concrete history. Further, in a book titled *Fundamental Buddhism*,[13] he attempted to identify the authentic sermons of Shakyamuni in the original Pali canon.

However, there had already been others before that who advocated the idea that the Mahayana is not the words of the Buddha. One such person was Nakamoto Tominaga (1715–46).[14] He was born into an Osaka family whose business for many generations had been the production of soy sauce. But his father was unusually fond of learning, and under his influence, Nakamoto set his heart on learning. He became the Confucian scholar of the town, had disciples, wrote several kinds of books, and did some publishing. He died at thirty-one due to a weak constitution, but his literary talent was such that he became quite famous and influential.

His most remarkable characteristic is that he was full of critical spirit. The rise of the merchant class after the Genroku period (1688–1703), and the new climate of freedom among Osaka merchants in particular, probably contributed to his critical spirit. In any case, Nakamoto's grasp of Confucianism and Buddhism from the perspective of historical development, and his critical attention to prior traditional scholarly research, were certainly remarkable. Though he lived in what was still the early modern period, in his attitude toward scholarship he already had a foot in the late modern period.

In *Emerging from Meditation*,[15] his most characteristic book, he proposed the theory of "development through accumulation."[16] This is the idea that theories and ways of thought develop historically, in the sense that once a particular idea or theory is established, another distinct idea or theory is added in order to surpass it. Thus, theories and ways of thought continuously develop through history. In other words, new theories are always arising throughout history, piling up one on top of the other. This theory, when applied to Buddhist sutras, makes many of them into products of "development through accumulation," which were not taught by Shakyamuni during his lifetime, but produced and added one to another during an orderly process of historical development. From this perspective, Nakamoto brought an historical order to the formation of the sutras.

In the first chapter of *Emerging from Meditation*, "The Sequence in which the Teachings Arose," Nakamoto says that before Shakyamuni, there were non-Buddhist teachings and that Shakyamuni founded Buddhism by adding to and complementing such teachings. And after the death of Shakyamuni, the three baskets of Buddhist scriptures were compiled—the teachings of the Buddha, the precepts and rules of the monastic community, and the commentaries on the teachings—which led to the appearance of Small Vehicle Buddhism. Subsequently, followers of Manjushri Bodhisattva created the wisdom (*prajna*) teachings by adding to the Small Vehicle. Then, one after another, there appeared groups devoted to the Lotus, Garland, Nirvana, and Lankavatara (the Sudden School) sutras, as well as esoteric groups, which are collectively called Mahayana Buddhism. Thus, he concluded that it is ignorant of Buddhist scholars to consider all of these teachings to be authentic words of Shakyamuni.

In the remaining chapters of the book, Nakamoto comments in detail on these teachings and theories, pointing out various divergences and discrepancies in them and spelling out how impossible it is to think that Shakyamuni, alone, had taught all of them. He indicates that Buddhist scholars' so-called "hermeneutic understanding of doctrine" was a far-fetched interpretation, used in order to make consistent the discrepancies and divergent theories that come with regarding them to be Shakyamuni's teachings and ideas. He was very critical of Tiantai Zhiyi's classification of the teachings into five chronological periods. Zhiyi placed all of the teachings or sermons that Shakyamuni had preached throughout his lifetime into five chronological periods, thereby giving an order to all of the sutras, and ranking the Lotus Sutra, which he placed in the fifth period, as the highest and ultimate teaching.

Nakamoto regarded only a small portion of the Agama sutras[17] to be authentic sermons of Shakyamuni. The Agama sutras were transmitted orally until they were written down long after Shakyamuni's death. Accordingly, Nakamoto made the logical claim that, since the verse (*gatha*) portions of the sutras were more suitable for oral recitation, the main body of a sutra is found there. His was a surprisingly great achievement, in that such insight and investigation into the formation of sutras is consistent with what modern research has now verified.

The theory that Mahayana Buddhism is not the words of the Buddha had been proposed long before in India and China, but in those cases it was mainly a matter of resistance to the Mahayana by Small Vehicle Buddhists. That is, Mahayana Buddhists called their school the "great vehicle" (*mahayana*) for attaining the truth and regarded other Buddhist schools as the "small vehicle." Thus was born the term Hinayana, or Small Vehicle. Small Vehicle Buddhists were naturally resistant to being crowned with this name and countered their opponents by using the theory that the Mahayana is not the words of the Buddha.

Thus developed the theory that Mahayana is not the words of the Buddha, and not as a result of the kind of scientific, verifiable approach that

Nakamoto would take. It is no exaggeration to say that the verifiable, scientific claim that Mahayana is not the words of the Buddha began with Nakamoto. In any case, his approach to investigation was a first in the history of Buddhist studies, a hundred years earlier than the textual criticism in Christianity arose in Europe.

Nakamoto also pointed out that individual subjective thinking influences thought and language, which appear differently according to the influences of the age, the society, and the regional ethos. He says, "In language there is a person. In language there is a world. In language there is variety." And to sum this up, "In language there are three things."[18] The expression "In language there is a person" means that how anything is understood and expressed depends on personal character. Accordingly, thought tends to be colored by personal bias. "In language there is a world" means that thought and language change with changes in society. And "In language there is variety" means that words differ in meaning depending on the time and place of their use, which he goes on to classify as five types. He calls the entire proposition "three things and five varieties."

Concerning the influence of the regional ethos, Nakamoto claimed that the characteristic ethos of India, for example, lay in its "fantasy" and that it was according to this reliance on fantasy that Buddhist sutras were produced there. Here "fantasy" means without limits. The word was used by Indian non-Buddhists and is similar to a Buddhist term meaning "supernatural." This use of "fantasy" was the driving force behind the various kinds of imaginative thought and expression that were brought together in order to produce the Buddhist sutras. An apt example of fantastic fantasy is found in the proclamation that Shakyamuni is the Everlasting Original Buddha, made in the sixteenth chapter of the Lotus Sutra.

By the way, "letters" characterize the Chinese ethos, while "conciseness" characterizes the Japanese ethos. The Chinese favor eloquence and rhetoric, while the Japanese favor simplicity and straightforward expressions. Since Nakamoto said that "Confucians indulge in 'letters,' and Buddhists indulge in 'fantasy,'" it appears that he preferred the "conciseness" of the Japanese. Yet, he was also critical of the Japanese, saying that their greatest fault is that they too highly value the esoteric and have a tendency to conceal things. In ancient times the Japanese were gentle, but under the influence of

Shinto and the performing arts, which were prominent from medieval to early modern times, the Japanese lifestyle, schools, and so forth seemingly grew more strict, and systems of exclusive transmission and instruction were established. Nakamoto lamented this as a derailment of the way of sincerity.

Several books were written from the Buddhist side to refute Nakamoto's *Emerging from Meditation* when it was first published. Yet anti-Buddhists of the time, who were rising in prominence, cherished his work. The Confucian scholar Tenyu Hattori (1724–69)[19] was motivated by it to write a volume called *Nakedness,*[20] which criticized Buddhism in a way similar to Nakamoto. In addition, the Japanese classical scholar Atsutane Hirata[21] wrote a four-volume work, *Laughter Following Meditation,*[22] in which he mimicked Nakamoto's *Emerging from Meditation* and ridiculed Buddhism in crude and unrefined ways. Atsutane wrote movingly in this book that he had tried in every way possible to find Nakamoto's *Emerging from Meditation,* after reading that Norinaga Motoori (1730–1801) had recommended reading the book in his eight-volume *Treasury of Essays.*[23]

Return to Early Buddhism

As previously stated, the theory that Mahayana is not the words of the Buddha appeared in Buddhist circles after European and modern research methods were introduced into Japan during the Meiji period. Buddhist scholars who wanted to study original Buddhist texts and do historical research on Buddhist scriptures introduced the idea. Because some of those scholars were themselves priests, criticizing the Mahayana scriptures revered within the very schools to which they belonged, and in which they earned their daily bread, was taboo. So they were reluctant to listen to and even closed their eyes to the theory that Mahayana is not the words of the Buddha. Some frowned upon such criticism. Among Buddhist scholars were some who, though they belonged to a school, agreed with the theory that Mahayana is not the words of the Buddha in their academic studies, yet adhered to traditional authority when returning to speak in sectarian contexts.

According to the theory that Mahayana is not the words of the Buddha, however, early Buddhist sutras are held to be the very words of Buddha— the authentic words of Shakyamuni. Thus, one could hear among Buddhist scholars of the time a call for a return to early Buddhism. The terms "early Buddhist sutras"[24] and "early Buddhism"[25] have been used since Meiji times. "Early Buddhist sutras" refer to the Pali scriptures that came to be known during the Meiji period through Chinese translations of the Agama sutras—traditionally regarded as the Small Vehicle sutras—and through studies by European scholars.

The Pali scriptures were transmitted to Sri Lanka and throughout South East Asia. In Japan they have been referred to as "The Great Collection of Sutras Transmitted in the South." The sutra portion of the three baskets (*sutra, vinaya, abhidharma*) consists of five collections (*nikayas*): the Long Discourses, (Digha-nikaya), the Middle Length Discourses (Majjhikma-nikaya), the Connected Discourses (Samyutta-nikaya), the Numerical Discourses (Anguttara-nikaya), and Miscellaneous Discourses (Khuddaka-nikaya).

The Chinese versions of the Agama sutras were transmitted from northwest India, via Central Asia, Nepal, and so on, to China, where they were translated into Chinese (the northern tradition). We assume that the original texts were written mainly in Sanskrit. The Sanskrit term agama means "traditional teaching." The Chinese Agama sutras consist of four sets of texts: the Long Discourses, the Middle Length Discourses, the Numerically Arranged Discourses, and Miscellaneous Discourses. These four, though not identical with them, correspond to four of the five Pali nikayas just mentioned.

The term "early Buddhism" refers to the Buddhism of the time when these early sutras were completed. Small Vehicle Buddhists devotedly followed these early sutras. However, since these sutras were completed prior to the period when Small Vehicle Buddhists split into several sects, thus falling into discord, the period in which the early sutras were formed, called the age of early Buddhism, is distinguished from it and placed at the beginning of the historical development of Buddhism. The period of sectarian division is considered to be the period of Small Vehicle Buddhism.

Some Buddhist scholars called the period of Shakyamuni and his disciples "fundamental Buddhism" and placed it in the preeminent position, and so Buddhism came to be classified into fundamental, early, Small Vehicle, and Mâhayana. But since "Hinayana" (Small Vehicle) is a pejorative term used by Mahayana Buddhists, and the peoples of Sri Lanka and Southeast Asia still believe in this form of Buddhism, these days it is called "sectarian" Buddhism to avoid using the pejorative term.

The formative periods of Buddhism are presumed to be approximately as follows. First, with respect to the dates of Shakyamuni's birth and death, there are now two leading theories, one favoring the dates of approximately 560–480 BCE, the other favoring the dates of approximately 460–380 BCE. In the case of the former, the period of early Buddhism is supposed to have lasted for about 250 years, until the time of King Ashoka. According to the latter theory, it is supposed to have lasted for only about 150 years.

Buddhism began to split into sects during the time of King Ashoka. When this dividing ended 150 years later, around the first century BCE, about twenty different so-called sects had been established. So this period is called the period of sectarian (Small Vehicle) Buddhism. The disputes that arose among the various sects during that period gave rise to the creation of new treatises on *abhidharma*.

Reform movements opposed to the Buddhism that had existed until that time arose around the beginning of the Common Era. This was Mahayana Buddhism, and from approximately that time on we have the so-called period of Mahayana Buddhism. Sectarian Buddhism did not disappear with the coming of Mahayana but continued to exist alongside, and occasionally opposed to, Mahayana Buddhism, as the latter grew in influence. As will be discussed in the next section, the development of Mahayana Buddhism is divided into four periods, and specific, so-called Mahayana sutras were produced or significantly enlarged in each of these periods.

When viewed from the perspective of the scheme of periodization, as "early Buddhist sutras," the original Pali text versions of the Agama sutras or their Chinese translations become the earliest Buddhist sutras. And these, accordingly, must be the words of the Buddha, being the closest to the period of Shakyamuni. In contrast, the Mahayana sutras, which were produced around the beginning of the first century, naturally come to be seen as not being the words of the Buddha. Thus, the theory that Mahayana is not the words of the Buddha prevailed. Meanwhile, the call to return to early Buddhism developed, and research on early sutras flourished.

The Meaning of the Words of the Buddha

As recent research on early sutras has progressed, the idea that these early sutras, because they are the earliest, are the words of the Buddha has become suspect. Among the early sutras, the Pali sutras had been thought to be earlier than the Agama sutras that exist in Chinese translation, but research comparing the two has revealed that this is not necessarily so. Research has found that some components of the Pali sutras were formed somewhat later than the Agama sutras. In addition, there are definite indications that some components of both the Pali sutras and the Agama sutras were formed after the early Mahayana sutras.

If this is so, the conviction that early sutras are the earliest, and thus the words of Buddha, cannot be firmly established. To be sure, among the early sutras there are a few that seem to be the earliest. But even within these seemingly earliest ones, analysis of the terms in them suggests that some parts were added later. Thus it is extremely difficult not only to maintain that the early sutras as a whole are the earliest, but to identify definitively the earliest parts within them, as well. Given these facts, it would be ridiculous to claim that the early sutras are the words of the Buddha.

Thus, even if we return to early Buddhism or to the early sutras, we reach the conclusion that we cannot confidently say that they are the earliest, or the words of the Buddha. If it is said that Mahayana is not the words of the Buddha, the same has to be said of the early sutras. Amazingly, Nakamoto Tominaga and Tenyu Hattori had already pointed this out. Nakamoto concluded that we can find something close to Shakyamuni's words in the Agama sutras, but only in a few chapters. Following him, Tenyu argued that "Even many Small Vehicle sutras were, to a large extent, produced at the hands of people of a later period. Rarely are many authentic words of the Buddha within them."[26] Moreover, since they did not have the tools for doing so decisively, the authentic parts were not clearly identified.

When one hears the term "sutra," something written immediately comes to mind. But this was not originally so. As Nakamoto says, Shakyamuni's disciples transmitted his words through memorization. The Buddhist sutras were conveyed from mouth to mouth. After Shakyamuni's passing, several meetings were held to compile the Buddhist teachings. For a while these meetings were convened for the purpose of verifying, through oral recitation, what had been memorized. According to legend, when Mahinda, the son of King Ashoka, was ordered to take Buddhism to Sri Lanka around the first century, some of the scriptures were written for the first time. As a result, the Pali sutras came into being.

Buddhist expressions were carved in the Brahmi and Kharoshthi scripts on King Ashoka's stone pillars, but this does not mean that Buddhist sutras were already written down by the time of King Ashoka. We presume that the Pali language was established around the first century BCE, that Buddhist scriptures were first written in Pali, and that they were brought to the South and first appeared in writing there. Yet the Pali language does not have its own alphabet or characters, but has been written in the scripts of South Asian countries, such as Sri Lanka, Burma, Thailand, and Cambodia. The script of these South Asian countries, in turn, originated from the expressions carved in stone in Brahmi script.

Since the words of the Buddha were handed down through memorization in the beginning, they were likely put into a form that could easily be memorized. Such forms as rhymed gathas or verses were used, as Nakamoto said. Based on this, we surmise that the verse portions of sutras were typically formed prior to the prose portions. But since Shakyamuni himself did not teach in rhymed verse, we cannot conclude that the verse portions are the authentic words of Shakyamuni, just because they are earlier. Rather, the problem lies in transmission through memorization. Memorization is not necessarily less accurate than writing, but during the time when the memorized materials were being handed down, the meanings of expressions would have changed depending on how they were understood, such that, in the long run, meanings quite different from those of the original expression may have emerged. In fact, there are many among the early sutras that emerged from distinct schools that revered different sutras.

Another reason for there being so many early sutras lies in Shakyamuni's way of teaching. We think that he did not teach fixed doctrine but rather according to his audience's ability to understand; that is, according to a person's capacity. So a variety of teachings emerged that were eventually compiled into diverse sutras.

As far as texts are concerned, the Pali texts were put into their present form around the fifth century, when Buddhaghosha travelled to Sri Lanka and compiled them. We should be able to distinguish earlier sutras from later ones, but as mentioned earlier, materials thought to be from later generations are mixed in with them. There are some Mahayana manuscripts among the many copies of Sanskrit originals recently discovered in places such as Central Asia and Nepal, which appear to be old. The manuscript of the Lotus Sutra discovered at Gilgit in Kashmir is one example, but it doesn't date back to earlier than the fifth or sixth century.

Most of the Sanskrit originals of these texts were written in the Gupta script, which was based on the Brahmi script used in the time of King Ashoka in the third century BCE. Gupta script was used in northern India beginning in the fourth century. The script that we usually see Sanskrit written in today is called Devanagari, which was derived from the Nagari family of scripts around the tenth century. The Siddham script, which was brought to Japan via China in the seventh century, was derived from the Gupta script, supposedly after the sixth century.

The translation of sutras did not begin in China until the second century, so the texts on which they were based were much earlier. But since they no longer exist, we cannot consider them here.

As indicated earlier, even if we were to return to early Buddhism, we would be faced with the incredible difficulty in finding authentic words of the Buddha and discover that it is impossible to do so. Thus we can say that early Buddhism is not the words of the Buddha for the same reasons that Mahayana Buddhism is not the words of the Buddha. In the end, we may feel a sense of desperation, given that Buddhism as a whole is not the teaching of Shakyamuni Buddha.

But in recent years a new tendency has emerged in which an attempt is made to reaffirm the faith of Buddhism by reinterpreting the meaning of "the words of the Buddha." Accordingly, "the words of the Buddha" need not necessarily be understood to be Shakyamuni's exact words but should be taken as what he truly meant. In other words, since terms and expressions vary from time to time depending on changes in society, the important thing is to address the content we have received via the vessels of words and expressions—that is, the ideas.

Two ways of thinking about or studying Buddhism emerge from this point of departure. The first is to dig down to the common stream that underlies the various sutras and forms of Buddhism to find what is called the fundamental spirit of Buddhism, the heart of Buddhism, or the teachings of Shakyamuni Buddha. Accordingly, the different sutras and schools of Buddhism boil down to nothing more than differences of expression due to differences in time, society, and level of understanding. The second way of thinking about Buddhism is to seek the depths of Buddhist thought. Even if Mahayana Buddhism, for example, was formed much later than the early and sectarian forms of Buddhism, if it conveys an authentic intent of Shakyamuni Buddha, we can say that it is truly the words of the Buddha.

Among those who long ago supported the first of these positions was Sensho Murakami (1851–1929)[27] of the Otani sect of Pure Land Buddhism. He wrote *A Treatise on the Unification of Buddhism*,[28] which advocated the idea that Mahayana is not the words of the Buddha while attempting to unify the various forms of Buddhism by making use of fundamental Buddhism. Because of this, he was excommunicated at one time. Yet his theory that Mahayana Buddhism was not the words of the Buddha was not intended to be a repudiation of the Mahayana. He was seeking, rather, to ferret out the underlying fundamental ideas shared in common by the various sutras and sects of Buddhism, in order to find Buddhism's fundamental essence, and thus to unify it.

Such a way of thinking is very reasonable. Yet it assumes that a common stream deeply underlies the various sutras and sects, so that it is possible for all of them to amount to the same thing. This conclusion is not the result of examination of the sutras but an assumption. Thus there is a limit to this kind of thinking. In fact, there are cases in which fundamentally incompatible or opposing things emerged between different sutras and sects. If this is the case, in the end we have to follow the second of the two ways of thinking about Buddhism. That is, it is only through deep reflection that we can argue and confront one another in order to seek the authentic intent of Shakyamuni Buddha.

Yet this second approach faces a different problem: on what basis can the depth of reflection be judged? Subjective opinions will probably influence such judgments. What's more, as it is, even deep reflection may not necessarily yield Shakyamuni Buddha's authentic intent. We lack adequate objective materials for regarding something as the authentic intent of Shakyamuni Buddha.

This being the case, the discussion veers the other way again, and we might once again give up out of desperation, or close our eyes and withdraw into the shell of traditional, sectarian doctrine. After all, religion is a crystallization of thinking, and while thought should be objective, in the end one has to choose according to one's own convictions. This applies to Buddhism and Buddhist sutras as well. Yet, in order to avoid ending up with something purely subjective and arbitrary, we should take as objective a perspective as is possible, and try to look at things objectively. In the end, this will lead to discussions, conversations, and personal associations, in particular, that transcend sect, as well as to a reevaluation of Buddhism from a contemporary standpoint.

Whatever the case may be, since it is now obvious that the various forms of Buddhism and sutras are all products of development, the only option that remains is to accept them as they are while objectively tracing their development, clarifying the character of their thought, and selecting which we are to follow. We might find something common among them as a result of this kind of process.

2

The Process of Formation of the Lotus Sutra

The Rise of Mahayana Buddhism

CHAPTER 4 OF the Lotus Sutra, "Faith and Understanding," begins with a confession by the Buddha's disciples, which includes the following noteworthy words:

> The World-Honored One has been preaching the Dharma for a long time, and all the while we have been sitting in our places, weary of body and mindful only of emptiness, formlessness, and non-action. Neither the enjoyments nor the divine powers of the bodhisattva-dharma—purifying buddha-lands and saving living beings—appealed to us.[29]

Here the weary disciples refer to Small Vehicle Buddhists. What is expressed is that they had fallen into a nihilistic way of life and had lost their desire to live.

Emptiness, formlessness, and nondoing (nonaction) were respected from ancient times as three gates to awakening, three gates to emancipation. Later they were symbolized in the gates of Buddhist temples and signified limitlessness, formlessness, and nonintention. They express the true nature of things, a summary of Shakyamuni's teaching, the basic structure of Buddhist truth, and, in the end, the kind of state of being that we should attain and practice. In this sense, there is nothing wrong with these. Yet there is a problem in the way that Small Vehicle Buddhists understood them nihilistically.

Among these three gates to emancipation, emptiness[30] (*shunyata*) was taken as basic. This is a result of observing the reality of things in the actual world as they are and of Dharma as their ground. Within the context of Western philosophy, Shakyamuni's position on observing reality or truth seems to me to be closest to modern phenomenology, or to existentialism, which more or less came from phenomenology. The motto of phenomenology is "to things themselves" (*zu den Sachen selbst!*). A German Indologist, Helmuth von Glasenapp, is said to have described Shakyamuni's position as phenomenological, based on the idea of dharma in early Buddhism.

Existentialism is a philosophy derived from a phenomenological position and is critical of essentialist philosophy. Essentialism arbitrarily presupposes the reality of essences unrelated to existence, and its ultimate aim is to return to essences. On the other hand, existentialism rejects all arbitrary judgments and presuppositions and directly seeks present human existence. Thus, existence, *Existenz, existentia* (i.e., the real thing), is taken to be prior to the essential, *essentia*, and thus existentialism supersedes essentialism. We could say that Shakyamuni's position on observing truth expressed in the phrase "knowing things as they are" is related to phenomenology and existentialist philosophy.

In fact, Shakyamuni criticized the philosophy of Brahmanism for making *brahman* the supreme principle of the cosmos and *atman* (individual soul) the immanent principle, and for reducing everything to them. He took observation of things as they are as his own starting point. Consequently, what he teaches is the impermanence of all things, the nonexistence of a permanent self, and interdependent arising. In other words, neither things nor the truth that is their basis are independent or unchanging, but always occur and change in relation to others. Such a way of occurring or being is, in a word, emptiness.

After the death of Shakyamuni, while his teachings were being sorted out, for the most part differences in thinking tended to be divided into two groups. According to the first, past, present, and future were actual, while the reality of Dharma was everlasting. That is, actual things change, appear, and disappear in relation to other things, while the truth (the Dharma)— being the ground of things, that which is the basis of actual things—was real and everlasting throughout the past, present, and future. According to the second way of thinking, only the present was real, not the past or the future. Small Vehicle Buddhists, who argued among themselves and were divided into several sects, are also characterized as mainly having these two kinds of thinking with respect to ontology or views of truth. They used increasingly precise arguments to support these two ways of thinking.

If I had to say which of these two ways of thought best matched Shakyamuni's basic position, it would be the latter, I think. This is because Shakyamuni rejected thinking based on the essential substantiality of something unchanging and imperishable. Yet some, having pursued the latter way of thinking to its end, ended up insisting that nothing existed even in the present: it was not only the variety of externally appearing phenomenal things but the inner truth as their ground or basis that did not really exist throughout the past, present, and future.

Thus they came to understand emptiness to mean the nothingness of all things and the fact that everything comes to nothing. It is said that Mahayana Buddhism was a successor to this way of thinking but that it firmly rejected understanding emptiness in such a nihilistic way. This rejection became the driving force behind the rise of Mahayana Buddhism. The appearance of the Lotus Sutra was part of the same development.

Mahayana Buddhism arose, around the beginning of the Christian era, as a kind of religious reform movement within Buddhism. It criticized the Buddhism up to that time (sectarian Buddhism) as a small vehicle (*Hinayana*) for attaining truth. With respect to the two ways of thinking above, the first maintained that things or matter can be analyzed into elements, which finally came to be seen as being real. This is nothing if not opposed to the fundamental position of Shakyamuni. On the other hand, the second view held that things can be analyzed into elements in the same way, but in its case they ultimately came to be seen as empty nothingness.[31] The second way of thinking turned out to be the opposite of the first in terms of its conclusions, but its way of conceiving the search for truth to be manipulative was the same as that of the first, so it fell into the empty nothingness mode of thought. This position later came to be called "the view that analyzes material things into emptiness," or more briefly, the "analysis into emptiness view," where "emptiness" is understood to mean nothingness.

Mahayana Buddhism strongly rejected understanding emptiness as nihilistic nothingness,[32] claiming that it was against the fundamental spirit of Shakyamuni and had lost sight of our ability to become a buddha. Voices were raised, therefore, saying that the two Hinayana vehicles could not lead to becoming a buddha. The term "two vehicles" here refers the two types of Hinayana Buddhists: the *shravakas* or voice-hearers—those who approached awakening through hearing Shakyamuni's teachings; and the *pratyekabuddhas* or self-enlightened ones—those who approached awakening on their own by observing within life and nature the appearance of causes and conditions and of coming into existence and passing away. For the most part, both fell into nihilism and lost the meaning and purpose of life. As a consequence, they regarded the state of awakening (*nirvana*) to be a return to nothingness by shutting oneself off from this world. Thus they lost any motivation for practical and socially constructive activity, and felt unhappy when they saw active people devoting themselves to such things. In other words, they became a kind of living dead. Such Hinayana nihilists were said to be people who could not become buddhas, as though the seed for growing into a buddha had been scorched.

In addition, a variety of other terms critical of Hinayana thought appeared at this time: such phrases as "bodies of ashes and dead wisdom," "salvation through solitary training," "seeing emptiness as nihilistic nothingness," and so forth. In brief, Mahayana Buddhists sharply criticized Hinayana Buddhists for going against the teachings of Shakyamuni. We might say that such criticism hits the target.

As for terms appropriate to nihilism, there were such original words as *venayika* and *nastika*. But if we look at the early sutras we see Shakyamuni described in this way:

> Some say: "The recluse Gautama is a nihilist (*venayika*); he teaches the annihilation, the destruction, the extermination of an existing being." As I am not, as I do not proclaim, so I have been falsely misrepresented thus.... Both formerly and now what I teach is suffering and the cessation of suffering.[33]

Perhaps he was a nihilist in the eyes of the Brahman philosophers of that time. This passage seems to be a defense against them.

We can see that Shakyamuni was not a nihilist and his teachings not nihilistic in the way that those who advocated theories of complete extinction (*uccheda-vada*) and nihilism (*natthika-vada*) in the early sutras were representative of the type that liberal thinkers of the time identified and criticized as the most typically non-Buddhist. As mentioned earlier, the nobility of the highest caste, the *brahmans*, did not show any interest in the actual world but were preoccupied with the idea of the supreme and absolute principle of *Brahman-Atman*. They regarded *Brahman-Atman* as pure and unmixed being, as reality. They saw the world of actuality, on the other hand, as mixed, transient, and inauthentic, and what's more, as not real. They taught that it is ultimately illusion (*maya*).

By the time Shakyamuni appeared in the fifth century BCE, the second and third castes, the *kshatriyas* (warriors and rulers) and the *vaishyas* (merchants and artisans), had arisen with their own powers for opening up the social system. Many liberal thinkers appeared with the support of these castes. Such thinkers, being rooted in the actual world, were naturally skeptical about the *brahman* caste's essentialist way of thinking. Some of them even held that the monistic *Brahman-Atman*, the idealistic realm of essences, was the real illusion, and that the pluralistic and material realm of phenomena was what was real.

Among these liberal thinkers there were six typical ones called the "six non-Buddhist teachers." Their positions varied from dualism to pluralism and included sensualist, mechanistic, and materialistic views. Some of these thinkers had even fallen from skepticism about the essentialist philosophy of the *brahmans* into pessimistic and nihilistic thinking. Shakyamuni came from a royal family of the Shakya clan. Magadha, the central place for his preaching, was a newly thriving urban area that arose with the development of commerce and industry, aided by which Shakyamuni took a position against the thinking of the *brahman* caste. But this does not mean that he was on the side of such liberal thinkers as the six non-Buddhist teachers. He rejected these non-Buddhist views as being trapped in delusion as well.

Shakyamuni rejected the philosophies of both the *brahmans* and the six non-Buddhist teachers. Once again he made his own clarification of reality and investigation of truth. Thus were born the teachings of "the impermanence of all things" (*anitya*), "the nonexistence of an enduring self" (*anatman*), and "emptiness" (*shunyata*), or "interdependent arising" (*pratitya-samutpada*). Shakyamuni regarded essentialist theories of reality, such as the *brahman* philosophy, as enamored with thinking of being (substantialism or eternalism), and regarded the nihilistic theory of complete extinction—the idea that death is the end of life—found among the non-Buddhist philosophers, as enamored with thinking of nothingness (annihilation at death and nonbeing). He said that he himself went beyond both positions and taught the Dharma. For example, the early Katyayanagotra Sutra[34] says:

> "All exists": Katyayana, is the one extreme. "All does not exist": this is the second extreme. Without veering toward either of these extremes, the Tathagata teaches the Dharma by the middle.[35]

And these words of criticism appear in chapter 2 of the Lotus Sutra, "Skillful Means":

> And [they] entered into a dense forest of wrong views about existence and nonexistence and the like.[36]

Thus, we know that Shakyamuni rejected both kinds of thinking—that of being and of nonbeing—as obstinate and one-sided.

To think that there is something independent, fixed, unchangeable, and immortal, such as a supreme and absolute God, a principle, a self, or pure mind or soul, and so forth, is to be prejudiced and deluded. Such are the views of enduring substance, being, or self. Shakyamuni, negating them, proposed the theories of "the impermanence of all things," "the nonexistence of an enduring self," and "interdependent arising." But "the impermanence of all things" and "the nonexistence of an enduring self" do not mean that everything changes, dies, and amounts to nothing. Such nihilistic thinking is simply the flipside of views of enduring substance or being. It amounts to the same clinging to delusion. It is a view that sees things as annihilated at death and as empty, in contrast to seeing them as enduring substances or as being.

For example, while discussions of whether there is life after death or whether the world exists or not are quite common, we know that arguments for existence, on the one hand, and for nonexistence, on the other, are of the same kind. People vigorously pursued such arguments about existence and nonexistence during Shakyamuni's time. It is said, however, that when such questions were put to him, he did not answer them. This was his nonresponse. If we say something *is*, that may be taken to be a kind of clinging to the illusion of being. But if we say something *is not*, that may be taken to be a kind of clinging to the illusion of nonexistence. Both involve the same kind of clinging. Until the questioner's prejudice is cleared away, there is no way to answer such questions.

This is why the true purpose of Shakyamuni's teachings of the impermanence of all things, the nonexistence of an enduring self, and interdependent arising, or his emphasis on life as suffering, eliminate all fixed ideas, surmounting and transcending various dualistic extremes such as "permanent and transient," "being and nothingness," "pleasure and suffering," and so forth.

With respect to the problem of pleasure and suffering, the early sutras teach that Shakyamuni abandoned the extremes of suffering and pleasure—asceticism on the one hand and hedonism on the other—relying on the middle way. The nondual middle way, the state of awakening or *nirvana* at which Shakyamuni aimed, the real nature of existence that he elucidated, and the way of truth surmount and transcend these two extremes.

Emptiness is also expressed with other terms. This is true in the Lotus Sutra, where aside from "emptiness" the term "empty space"[37] is often used. This term expresses the absolutely infinite world that goes beyond all limits and boundaries. Thus, emptiness is not nothingness. Some Small Vehicle Buddhists fell into nihilism by confusing emptiness and nothingness. That certainly was a distortion of what Shakyamuni actually meant, and can be blamed for leading them into non-Buddhism. This is one more reason why there was heavy criticism of this point with the rise of Mahayana Buddhism.

One's thought may tend toward nihilism when confronted with impermanence or emptiness, so it is understandable that some Small Vehicle Buddhists thought in this way. Actually, it is very difficult to understand impermanence and emptiness in a way that directly overcomes nihilism, or to work one's way through nihilism by means of impermanence and nothingness. This is a matter of no small difficulty in existentialism as well.

Essentialist thinking lay behind Plato's theory of ideas in ancient Greece, behind the concept of God in Christianity, and behind Kant's teaching of "things-in-themselves" and Hegel's "absolute spirit" in modern thought. Nietzsche's cry of "God is dead!" overturned such traditional thinking and announced nihilism, bringing about a dramatic change in Western philosophy. Later Husserl developed his phenomenology, and even more so, Heidegger and others developed their existential philosophies. Existentialism began with skepticism and the negation of earlier essentialism. In this sense, Nietzsche's nihilism served as the medium for existentialism, just as the nihilism of the six non-Buddhist teachers served as the medium for Shakyamuni's skepticism with regard to *brahman* essentialism. Nietzsche himself pointed out that a thoroughgoing skepticism was prevalent in Shakyamuni's time.

Yet the aim of existentialism was to rediscover the truly absolute ground, and by so doing, to overcome despair and nihilism by experiencing the hopelessness of essentialism, as well as of the nihilism of Nietzsche. It is extremely doubtful that existentialists have succeeded in this. Escaping from despair and nihilism by working through them is tremendously difficult. Existentialism is a reflection of modern nihilistic conditions, rather than an escape from them. It is a philosophy of despair. This is why it is criticized for being bogged down in the depths of nihilism.

Yet the contemporary world can no longer return to an age in which we simply believe in the reality of God. There is only one way left for the contemporary world to rediscover God, and that is through despairing of God. That was true in Shakyamuni's time as well, and that is why his teachings often sounded as though they were despairing and nihilistic. But Shakyamuni himself was confident that he was bringing a gospel of salvation that would overcome despair and nihilism and cast a ray of hope. This is what he proclaimed.

Naturally, the idea of emptiness sounds nihilistic, in terms of the words that express it, but this is merely a result of its negation of the essentialist thinking of *brahmanism*. It actually shows itself to be the truly absolute foundation, which is just what Mahayana Buddhism hoped to express. Thus, trying at first to establish the principle of emptiness or its true meaning, and then to include it in the sutras being compiled at that time, Mahayana Buddhism came into being.

The Formation of Mahayana Sutras

In order to first understand the true meaning of emptiness, Mahayana Buddhists devoted themselves to elucidating its principles, which they included in the sutras then being compiled. Thus they developed the various "perfection of wisdom" (*prajnaparamita*) sutras, from the large to the small. It seems that the earliest ones were completed by around 50 CE and that others were gradually added. Consider the following words from the Perfection of Wisdom Sutra regarding emptiness:

> What is emptiness of form, that is not form; nor is emptiness other than form; the very form is emptiness, and the very emptiness is form.[38]

There is no extinction in emptiness and there is nothing to be extinguished. Things are ultimately emptiness—that is, they are nirvana.[39] The Vimalakirti Sutra,[40] a sutra of the same family, similarly teaches:

> Form is emptiness—it is not that form extinguishes emptiness but that the nature of form is of itself empty.[41]

That is, we will not be able to understand emptiness, or gain a good general idea of it by continually analyzing actual things (form) into abstractions, as if peeling away the layers of an onion. Emptiness, understood in such a way, is taken to mean nihilism. The truth is that emptiness can be experienced only in the midst of the dynamic movement of things as they are.

The Heart Sutra,[42] still much-read even now, teaches:

> Form is emptiness, emptiness is form; emptiness is not other than form, form too is not other than emptiness.

The expression "form is emptiness, emptiness is form" is so popular that it is recited phonetically in Japanese as "*shiki sokuze ku, ku sokuze shiki.*" Its meaning is as explained above.

Small Vehicle Buddhism analyzed things, came to see them finally as empty, and fell into nihilism. In contrast, Mahayana Buddhism viewed emptiness as in all things, just as they are. The Small Vehicle view of emptiness later came to be called "the view that analyzes things into emptiness," and the Mahayana view was designated as "the view that sees emptiness in all things." Tiantai Zhiyi, founder of Lotus philosophy, developed a detailed logic around this point.

We also find other important expressions concerning emptiness in the Perfection of Wisdom sutras, such as "emptiness is empty" and "emptiness too amounts to emptiness." "Emptiness is empty" means that there is no such thing as an emptiness that is a substantial reality over against things. In this sense, emptiness is also said to be empty. Small Vehicle Buddhists denied the reality of actual things, threw them out, and clung to emptiness, making of emptiness a kind of thing that is empty. This is contrary to the authentic meaning of emptiness and is typical of nihilism.

In nihilism, nothingness is tenaciously held to be a "no-thing"—a kind of thing. Such is nihilism. Small Vehicle Buddhists tenaciously clung to emptiness as a thing, and as a result they fell into nihilism. In order to correct such understandings, the idea that emptiness, too, is empty was taught.

Emptiness is not something to tenaciously cling to. Yet Small Vehicle Buddhists did tenaciously cling to emptiness and perversely stuck to an extremely one-sided view of it. In chapter 37 of the *Great Wisdom Discourse*,[43] a commentary attributed to Nagarjuna on the Great Perfection of Wisdom Sutra, such positions were labeled "emptiness only." In contrast, the Mahayana position was labeled "emptiness that is beyond words and thought" or "not only emptiness," terms that indicate being neither limited to emptiness nor taking an extremely one-sided position on it. In other words, Mahayana Buddhists holistically observed phenomena and actual things just as they are, defining the actual state of things as empty. So they understood that to grasp emptiness is actually to go out into the real world and put one's faith into practice by improving actual things. This is why Mahayana was said to be "not only emptiness." Because the true meaning of emptiness is found herein, the phrase "the wonderful reality of true emptiness" was born.

Nagarjuna[44] (ca. 150–250), who systematized thought about emptiness based on the Perfection of Wisdom sutras, in his *Verses on the Middle Way*[45] argues:

All is possible when emptiness is possible.
Nothing is possible when emptiness is impossible.[46]

Thus, all things are empty. In other words, all things are possible.

Further, we also have the term "nondual" (*advaita*), which applies the concept of emptiness to two relative things. This idea is so important that a whole chapter of the Vimalakirti Sutra—chapter 9, "The Dharma Gate of Nonduality"—is devoted to consideration of it. Let me explain it simply, with the example of the duality of man and woman. Neither male nor female exist as such as an independent and fixed reality. Rather, man exists only because woman does, and vice versa. Man exists as man in an interdependent relationship with woman, and vice versa. This is the true reality of the duality of man and woman. What it expresses is nonduality.

Thus, "emptiness" does not mean that various beings amount to nothing; one does not fall into nihilism if one understands it in this way. While the varieties of things are interrelated as a whole, each of them dynamically becomes, and it is just such a state, such a reality, that is called emptiness. In other words, to see emptiness from an epistemological and practical point of view is to observe various things as they are (objectively) and to observe them as a whole without clinging to one part. In this way, the practice of genuine, committed subjectivity emerges. This is what Shakyamuni meant by awakening. When put into a formula, it becomes: a view of the self as substantial (false subjectivity) combined with a view of things as substantial (false objectivity) leads to the emptiness of self (genuine subjectivity) and the emptiness of things (genuine objectivity).

The selfish view of the self is a matter of seeing the self as fixed and unchanging, as a kind of absolute, and then seeing and judging other things on that basis. In other words, it is false subjectivity; it is deluded and clinging. In reality, nothing like an unchanging, fixed, absolute self exists. In other words, the self is a self-less self or a self-emptying self. A self that sees itself as impermanent sees things as they are. To know the true appearance of the self as a self-less self or as a self-emptying self is to see things phenomenologically in accord with the way they are. It is, in brief, to be genuinely objective.

The selfish view of things involves seeing things as fixed and unchanging and then clinging to them. It is, in brief, a false objectivity. It is also deluded and involves clinging. In reality no unchanging fixed things exist. In other words, things are without independent reality; they are empty of independent reality. To know the true appearance of things as being without independent reality is to have a phenomenological mind, one free from clinging to objects, and conversely to be able to participate in the reality of objects from a phenomenological or nonselfish perspective. In this way, emptiness is not a matter of falling into nihilism but of enabling both objects and the self to exist and live as they should.

With reference again to the example of the duality between man and woman, this means, on the one hand, that it is an error to regard the nonduality or emptiness of man and woman as meaning that either one is a fixed, unchanging, or absolute reality, or as meaning that one is subordinate to the other. On the other hand, it is also an error to see them as unrelated, independent, and fixed realities. Yet this does not mean that they are reduced to something like non-man or non-woman. It means, rather, that man as man and woman as woman fulfill the potential of their particular gender, and at the same time are one. Conversely speaking, man and woman are alive in their particular ways on the basis of their nonduality or emptiness. Zhanran (711–782),[47] the sixth patriarch of Tiantai, defined this relationship between the two as "nondual duality" or "the duality of nonduality." Here nonduality becomes dual and duality becomes nondual.

There is also the matter of referring to the Buddha as "Tathagata,"[48] which can be considered in connection to both the Sanskrit term *tatha-gata* and the Sanskrit term *tatha-agata*. The former means seeing the true state of things, reality, as it really is and becoming one with it. The latter means the reverse, coming out from such oneness into the actual world, bringing the truths grasped there into the world and liberally making use of them to save people. In Chinese translation, *tatha-gata* becomes *rulai*—that is, the Buddha is one who selflessly observes reality and truth, and with true objectivity makes practical use of it. Such a person is called a tathagata.

"Empty (*shunya*)" and "emptiness (*shunyata*)" were defined on the basis of the essence of this truth. When defined properly, they were called "oneness (*tatha*)"[49] and "without distinctions (*tathata*)."[50] In this case *tathagata* means to be or to become or to appear as it is. In other words, because the truth taught within Buddhism is grasped by seeing things as they are, it is called the truth of emptiness.

When we speak of the truth itself, we use the word *dharma*, the original meaning of which is "that which sustains things." For the reasons given above, this "dharma" was used quite often in Buddhism for that which points to things themselves. In any case, it was in this sense that emptiness was talked about. We should not understand or construe it in the sense of things being meaningless or in a nihilistic way. The term "emptiness" had already appeared in the early sutras, but it was taken up in a big way in Mahayana Buddhism. Mahayana Buddhists tried to correct the Small Vehicle construal of emptiness as nihility and to establish its true meaning. By doing so they developed ways of expressing emptiness positively and expanded Mahayana Buddhism. Various Mahayana sutras were produced along with this development.

As previously stated, the Perfection of Wisdom sutras were meant to establish the true meaning of emptiness and to explicate the principle involved. When this work had been mostly finished, subsequent efforts were made to express emptiness positively. The Lotus Sutra and the Flower Garland Sutra[51] appeared as a part of this process. It is believed that the earlier parts of the Lotus Sutra were formed around 50 CE, and the earlier parts of the Flower Garland Sutra somewhat later. After that, these sutras were gradually added to and grew to become what we have today.

For the most part, we can chronologically divide the formation of the main Mahayana sutras into four periods, corresponding in order to the formation of the Perfection of Wisdom sutras, the Vimalakirti Sutra, the Lotus Sutra, and the Flower Garland Sutra. These four, being the earliest, are regarded as the first of the Mahayana sutras (first to third centuries). Pure Land sutras, such as the Amitayus Sutra and Amitabha Sutra, also belong to this period.

The Lotus Sutra positively expresses the truth of emptiness. In it, integration into one cosmic truth (the Wonderful Dharma of One Vehicle) was also proposed, and on this basis many new things were worked out. In contrast, the Flower Garland Sutra is full of the idea that the truth of emptiness takes the form of pure oneness and describes a world reflected through this truth of pure oneness. The Lotus Sutra pursues an image of the cosmos integrated with the world, while the Flower Garland Sutra depicts an image of the ideal.

At the end of the second and beginning of the third centuries, Nagarjuna produced the *Verses on the Middle Way, Discourse on the Twelve Gates*,[52] the *Great Perfection of Wisdom Discourse*, and so on, in an attempt to create a new systemization of Mahayana Buddhism based on the idea of emptiness. His disciple, Aryadeva[53] (ca. 170–270), produced the *One Hundred*,[54] the *Four Hundred*,[55] and so on. The *One Hundred, Verses on the Middle Way*, and *Discourse on the Twelve Gates* are together called the "three treatises," or the "four treatises" when supplemented with the *Great Perfection of Wisdom Discourse*. In China, new schools, called "Three Treatise"[56] and "Four Treatise"[57] schools, arose around these texts.

In the fourth century, a group of sutras appeared in which another step was taken toward establishing the truth of emptiness positively as eternal and universal existence (the everlasting Dharma-body), covering in this way the whole of reality, and teaching the immanence of emptiness in reality (buddha nature or *tathagatagarbha*). These were the so-called Buddha Nature sutras. To name them mostly in chronological order, they are the Buddha Nature Sutra, the Discourse on Nonemerging and Nondisappearing Sutra, the Great Drum Sutra, the Angulimala Sutra, the Lion's Roar of Queen Shrimala Sutra (Shrimala Sutra), the Great Final Nirvana Sutra (Nirvana Sutra), the Sublime Shelter Sutra,[58] and others.

Meanwhile, in parallel with the Buddha Nature sutras, another group of sutras appeared that were concerned with the constantly emerging, passing away, and changing actual realities. These sutras posited a kind of foundational "store-consciousness"[59] as the principle for interpreting the occurrence of phenomena, and they analyzed phenomena on that basis. The Sutra of Understanding Profound and Esoteric Meaning and the Mahayana Abhidharma Sutra[60] are included in the family of Store-Consciousness sutras. The Buddha Nature sutras and the Store-Consciousness sutras are together categorized as being from the second period of Mahayana sutras (fourth century).

Asanga (ca. 310–390 CE) and his brother Vasubandhu (ca. 320–400) developed a theory based on the Store-Consciousness Sutras. Consciousness Only[61] philosophy emerged with them, and the Yogacara school developed in their wake. Subsequently, the Yogacara school sometimes came into conflict with the Middle Way (*Madhyamika*) school, based on Nagarjuna's conception of emptiness and the middle way.

Asanga wrote the *Compendium of the Mahayana*, the *Acclamation of Scriptural Discourse*, the *Abhidharma Digest*,[62] and others, and Vasubandhu wrote the *Twenty Verses*, the *Thirty Verses*, *Buddha Nature Treatise*, *Commentary on the Compendium of Mahayana*,[63] *Commentary on the Lotus Sutra*,[64] and others. Notable about Vasubandhu is the fact that in two or three of his writings he refers not only to store-consciousness but to buddha nature as well. This indicates the beginning of attempts to synthesize and unify the ideas of buddha nature and store-consciousness. By the fifth century, sutras that tried to integrate these two began to appear, such as the Journey to Lanka Sutra and Great Vehicle Mystic Adornment Sutra.[65] These are categorized as Mahayana sutras of the third period (fifth century).

The integration of the ideas of buddha nature and store-consciousness elucidates the relationship between what is everlasting, nonemerging, and nondisappearing (i.e., nonduality) on the one hand, and what actually emerges and disappears (duality) on the other, and tries to integrate them. It seems that this process reached a conclusion in *The Awakening of Faith in Mahayana*, believed to be a work of the sixth century. Though it is attributed to the second-century figure Ashvaghosha, by examining its content and style of exposition in terms of the logical coordination of buddha nature and store-consciousness, or of the everlasting with the actual, we know this work to be much more advanced than the Mahayana sutras of the third period. It seems reasonable to regard it as a work of the sixth century. Moreover, there is a strong case for regarding it as having been created at that time in China.

The esoteric Mahavairocana and Diamond Peak sutras[66] were created in India in the seventh century. They are considered to have incorporated Middle Way and Consciousness Only philosophies into esoteric teachings, the former sutra having been influenced by the Middle Way School, and the latter by the Consciousness Only School. These esoteric sutras are categorized as the fourth and final period in the development of the Mahayana sutras (seventh century). After that, Buddhism in India began to degenerate through syncretism with folk religions. Finally, in 1203 a Muslim army destroyed the Vikramashila Temple in central India, practically bringing Buddhism in India to an end. However, it was during this period that Buddhism, together with its various sutras, streamed into many places outside of India, where it survived and further developed.

The Formation of the Lotus Sutra

The Lotus Sutra in its present form has twenty-eight chapters. But since chapter 12, "Devadatta," did not appear as a separate chapter until the time of Tiantai Zhiyi in the sixth century, the sutra originally had only twenty-seven chapters.[67] Traditionally, the sutra was divided in two between chapters 14, "Safe and Easy Practices," and 15, "Springing Up from the Earth." But in modern times various attempts have been made to divide it according to research on and explication of original texts. If we now reexamine it with reference to these various divisions, the following seems reasonable: The part of the sutra that spans from chapter 2, "Skillful Means," through chapter 9, "Assurance for Arhats," can be seen as the first part, which we can assume to have been formed around 50 CE. Then the part that spans from chapter 10, "Teachers of the Dharma," through chapter 22, "Entrustment," together with the first chapter, "Introduction," can be regarded as the second part, which we may assume to be from around 100 CE. And finally, chapter 23, "Previous Lives of Medicine King Bodhisattva," through chapter 28, "Encouragement of Universal Sage Bodhisattva," can be seen as a third part, formed around 150 CE.

As previously stated, the first group of chapters, formed around 50 CE, is the original part of the Lotus Sutra. Later the second group was put together and added to the first. It seems that chapter 1, "Introduction," was created at that time and placed at the beginning in order to create some coherence between the first and second groups. I imagine that the third group was created after the formation of the second as a way of assimilating the general thought and faith that arose at that time. It seems that each of these chapters were created individually and then successively added to the sutra. The reason for regarding this third group to be from around 150 CE lies in the fact that citations from the Lotus Sutra, even from its last chapter, appear in the *Great Perfection of Wisdom Discourse*, written by Nagarjuna around 200 CE.

When we explore the division into first and second groups, we see that between chapter 9, "Assurance for Arhats" and chapter 10, "Teachers of the Dharma," the audience of Shakyamuni's sermon changes. Up to chapter 9, Shakyamuni addresses the shravakas, one of the two kinds of followers of the Small Vehicle, while from chapter 10 on, he addresses bodhisattvas. In chapter 1 as well, bodhisattvas are the audience. As discussed, chapter 1 was created at the time of the formation of the second group in order to provide coherence between the two groups of chapters.

Next, it is worth noting that in chapters 2–9 the Buddha gives individual assurances of becoming a buddha, while from the latter part of chapter 10 on he advocates social propagation of the Dharma. The assurance of becoming a buddha is meant mainly to signify that Small Vehicle shravakas are equally assured of becoming buddhas in the future, after being awakened and transformed by the Wonderful Dharma of One Vehicle. In general, "assurance" (*vyakarana*) refers to assurance by the Buddha that one will become a buddha in the future. The special entrustment, general entrustment, and the like signify the transmission of the Buddha's mission to those who put truth into actual practice, thereby propagating it in society. Such assurance symbolizes the paragon of Mahayana Buddhism and has a deep relationship with the Mahayana bodhisattvas.

In this context, we should think again about the location of the "Entrustment" chapter. This chapter is about entrusting the Dharma or the mission to others. It is placed last in all versions, except for the extant Sanskrit texts and Kumarajiva's translation. In Kumarajiva's translation it is located after chapter 21, "Divine Powers of the Tathagata." After examining the content and title of the chapter, I think this location is proper, as the chapter brings a long story and the second group of chapters to a conclusion.

In the chapters preceding "Teachers of the Dharma" (chapter 10), *stupas* are regarded as a place for relics of Shakyamuni, but later chapters emphasize stupas as a place for sutras. This change reflects both a criticism of the Small Vehicle monastic tradition for becoming absorbed in idealistic thought and a criticism of falling into nihilism. It is also reflects lay traditions of materialistic folk belief, seen in the worship of Shakyamuni's relics (*sharira*) or of the stupas that contained such relics. The sutra-holding stupa is said to be a result of the true spirit of the Mahayana bodhisattva way, which reflects and criticizes both monastics and laity, and synthesizes them.

In Japanese the term *bodhisattva* is usually translated phonetically as *bosatsu*.[68] *Bodhisattva* can also be translated as *kakuujo*,[69] which can be taken as meaning either "a person seeking (going toward) awakening" or "a person coming from awakening." When this word is used in contrast to the Small

Vehicle monks, the shravakas, it seems to have the latter meaning. That is, a bodhisattva is an awakened one who comes into this actual world and works so that awakening will be embodied within this society. This is generally the meaning of "bodhisattva" in Mahayana Buddhism, and it is what the second group of chapters in the Lotus Sutra emphasizes.

For these reasons we know that a division can be made between chapters 9 and 10, that the chapters from 10 to 21 were drawn up as a second group, and that they were then added to the group of chapters preceding 10. Then we can say that the purpose of creating this second group was to exalt the bodhisattva spirit and to promote the bodhisattva movement. For example, chapter 16, "The Lifetime of the Tathagata," which is part of the second group, has traditionally been interpreted as revealing Shakyamuni to be the Universal Buddha, as is stated in the text. I think it is significant, however, that it reveals the unceasing practice of the bodhisattva way to be the eternal life of the Buddha, thus emphasizing the bodhisattva way.

Here I want to mention briefly the chronological divisions involved in the formation of the Lotus Sutra. In the earliest part of the sutra the prose sections amplify the verse sections, or conversely, the verses repeat what is in the prose sections. This seems to indicate that the verse sections were created first and then the prose sections added to supplement them. On the other hand, in the second group of chapters there are many things in verse form that are not merely repetitions of what was in prose, and we can only make sense of the whole through a combination of the prose and verse sections. Therefore, we can imagine that in this case the prose and verse sections were created at the same time. In this respect, too, there seems to be some difference between the first and second groups of chapters.

Moreover, within the first group, the terms "receive and embrace," "read and recite," and "explain" occur regularly, but "copy" is not mentioned. "Copy" was added in the second group, completing the set that later came to be known as the five kinds of Dharma teacher practice—receive and embrace, read, recite, explain, and copy. Thus we see, again, a chronological difference between the first and second groups. The fact that "copy" is not mentioned in the first group is a vestige of the period of memorization prior to the development of writing in India, indicating that the first group is older.

Also, the six lower realms or paths—i.e., those of purgatories or hells, hungry spirits, animals, asuras, people, and heavenly beings—are found in the first group, but the idea of the ten realms of living beings, which include the realms of shravakas, pratyekabuddhas, bodhisattvas, and buddhas, was-not yet formulated. We see the ten realms, however, in the second group, which provides another reason for maintaining that there is a chronological division between the formation of the first and second groups. It was not until sometime after the beginnings of Mahayana Buddhism that the realms of shravakas, pratyekabuddhas, bodhisattvas, and buddhas were added to the six lower realms. Beyond this, there are several other reasons, in terms of contents and chronological period, for maintaining a distinction between the first and second groups of chapters.

Even though the second group was formed later than the first group, from the perspective of the original text of the Lotus Sutra as a whole, we can say that the second group, which emphasizes bodhisattva practice, is the heart of the sutra. Therefore, I want to look into each chapter of the second group in greater detail. First of all, when we look at chapter 10, "Teachers of the Dharma," the emphasis on bodhisattvas as apostles of the Buddha or Tathagata is remarkable. That is, those who receive and disseminate even a single phrase of Dharma after the death of the Buddha are regarded as apos-tles of the Buddha, commissioned by the Buddha to save all living beings in this world, and extolled as "apostles of the Tathagata."

The latter part of the chapter promotes entering the Tathagata's room, wearing the Tathagata's robe, sitting on the Tathagata's seat, and preach-ing Dharma without hesitation. The Tathagata's room, robe, and seat are said to be compassion, patience, and realization of the emptiness of things. Compassion involves treating others with affection and kindness. Patience means enduring without holding things against others. And realization of the emptiness of things means being freed from attachments and placing oneself within the vast and infinite world. These concisely express the atti-tude a follower of the bodhisattva way holds toward life. Later these came to be valued as the three ways of propagating the sutra.

For some Small Vehicle Buddhists, compassion is an act of being engaged with this world, while the realization of emptiness is a state that goes beyond it, and so compassion should be discarded in order to realize emptiness. But chapter 10 of the Lotus Sutra teaches the unity of compassion and emptiness.

We can understand from this that realization of emptiness is taken positively as a norm for practice in this world. Here too we can see an example of the positive understanding of emptiness found in Mahayana Buddhism.

In chapter 11, "The Sight of the Treasure Stupa," a jeweled stupa in which Abundant Treasures (Prabhutaratna)[70] Tathagata sits floats in mid-air. Shakyamuni Buddha goes from the ground to the stupa in the air and sits beside Abundant Treasures Buddha. With that, the buddhas who are embodiments or representatives of Shakyamuni Buddha come from various directions to be united with him, while at the same time, various worlds are united into a single buddha-land. Abundant Treasures is a buddha who appeared prior to Shakyamuni. One can understand that the two of them sitting side-by-side symbolizes that Shakyamuni has been a buddha from the very remote past—that is, it suggests the universality of Shakyamuni Buddha. The gathering together of the buddhas embodying Shakyamuni from throughout the universe and the common buddha-land express the idea that Shakyamuni Buddha is a unifying buddha.

In this sense, chapter 11 should be taken as a kind of prelude to chapter 16, "The Lifetime of the Tathagata." As in chapter 16, this chapter also emphasizes bodhisattva practice, advocates actual bodhisattva practice in the heart of this saha world during the last days, and teaches entrusting the Dharma to bodhisattvas. Thus, we ought to reexamine ideas such as the jewelled stupa rising up, the gathering together of buddha embodiments, and a common buddha-land from the perspective of promoting bodhisattva practice.

Chapter 13, "Encouragement to Uphold the Sutra," also teaches entrusting to bodhisattvas the mission of disseminating the Dharma in the evil age, and especially emphasizes the practice of martyrdom by bodhisattvas who are so entrusted. The chapter closes with bodhisattvas vowing to disseminate the Dharma despite intolerable suffering. Nichiren, who suffered many hardships in his life, and his followers, who were also believers in the Lotus Sutra, were encouraged and supported by this exaltation of the spirit of martyrdom, and by the teaching of "the apostles of the Tathagata" found in chapter 10. These teachings also gave them a sense of being among the religious elite and helped create strong bonds of communal friendship. Some contemporary scholars comment that this bodhisattva sense of being an apostle or a martyr is unique within Buddhism.

Because the Lotus Sutra generates such a bodhisattva spirit, some suspect that a distinct group produced it. Even if such a group did exist, since there is no concrete evidence for it, the idea that it existed is no more than conjecture. Rather, the bodhisattva spirit that the Lotus Sutra emphasizes was a radical version of the idea of the bodhisattva way that is generally found in Mahayana Buddhism. So it seems that we need not treat the Lotus Sutra as a special case.

As we will discuss later, in the fourth chapter of the Lotus Sutra, "Faith and Understanding," there appears the famous parable of the rich man and his poor son. The older rich man represents Shakyamuni Buddha and the poor son represents nihilistic Small Vehicle Buddhists. The story portrays the rich man as running a big business; when he is on his deathbed, even a king and his ministers gather around him. Some think that the fact that the man is very rich is intended as praise for the virtue and authority of Shakyamuni Buddha. But based on the fact that the Lotus Sutra portrays a man of wealth, we can imagine the kind of society to which its composers may have belonged: a society of commercial production. This, however, can be said not only of the group that produced the Lotus Sutra but of Mahayana Buddhists in general.

Small Vehicle Buddhists also had connections with men of property as sponsors or supporters, and maintained the sangha with their aid, but they rejected secular occupations personally, secluding themselves within monasticism. In contrast, Mahayana Buddhists situated themselves within society and probably affirmed the activities of everyday life. Thus we can imagine the development of a commercial economy to have been the background for the rise of Mahayana Buddhism. From about 50 CE the Kushana dynasty, centered in northern India, prospered with the help of trade with Rome and had a money-based economy and commercial production. The Mahayana Buddhist movement developed aggressively during that time.

Thus, Mahayana Buddhism or Mahayana Buddhists were closely related to commercial production, and that relationship appears in the Lotus Sutra. One piece of evidence for this is the way in which the Buddha is described as being like a wealthy man of property in chapter 4. Furthermore, although there are no direct references to commercial production in the Lotus Sutra, we might think of the words that affirm secular life in chapter 19 and elsewhere from the same perspective.

This is also illustrated by the many terrible persecutions that befall bodhi-sattvas in chapters 10 and 13. Furthermore, this kind of thing led people to believe that the Lotus Sutra came from a special group that was estranged from society. But since Mahayana Buddhists, in general, experienced such persecution, it was not limited to the Lotus Sutra group. As taught in the Lotus Sutra, those who did the persecuting or who instigated it were mainly Small Vehicle Buddhists or people on the side of Small Vehicle Buddhists. It has been suggested that such persecution occurred because the social position and background of Small Vehicle and Mahayana Buddhists were different, as we have seen.

Be that as it may, the social background of the Lotus Sutra group and the persecution that they suffered were common throughout Mahayana Buddhism, so it seems unnecessary to regard the Lotus Sutra group as having any special social status. Yet the term "apostle of the Tathagata" and con-sciousness of apostolic martyrdom were first based on the Lotus Sutra. So, in this respect, we can understand how one might feel that there is something unique about the Lotus Sutra. But since this feeling really has to do with the sutra's emphasis on bodhisattva practice, there is no need to understand it in some special way.

Incidentally, the bodhisattva way of chapter 14, "Safe and Easy Practices," is quiet and passive when compared to the previous chapter. For this reason some have seen it as being different in quality, and as having been inserted at a later time. From early times it has been interpreted as being inferior and taught for beginner bodhisattvas who cannot follow the difficult practices of martyrdom and self-sacrifice found in chapter 13. But the audience for this chapter was none other than bodhisattvas. Furthermore, the first part of the chapter advocates bodhisattva practice in the latter age. So it could well be thought of as a kind of follow-up to chapter 13. It teaches a quiet and passive bodhisattva practice because it advocates that followers of the bodhisattva way engage in self-reflection on practical knowledge and mis-sions, perhaps as a way of maintaining individual self-identity. It makes sense if we understand it in such a way.

In chapter 15, "Springing Up from the Earth," a group of bodhisattvas led by four, such as Bodhisattva Superior Practice,[71] emerge from this saha world and reveal themselves to be direct disciples of the Buddha. They are described as ones who, having been entrusted by him to do so, will disseminate the Dharma after the Buddha is gone. This may be an indication that those who struggle within actual society are especially authentic Buddhists.

It is explained that these bodhisattvas dwell below, in an empty space under this saha world. As we have seen earlier, this "empty space" is another name for emptiness, and the two terms are often used interchangeably. Thus, we can interpret "living in an empty space below this saha world" to mean that being grounded in an experience of emptiness, they remain in this saha world without clinging to it. In other words, chapter 15 criticizes the way of the holy ones, the shravakas, for transcending actual reality in order to stagnate in emptiness, thereby falling into nihilism. Instead, it highly values the figure of the ordinary person, the bodhisattva, who lives in the actual world, the temporal world, without getting bogged down in it, and works diligently, with emptiness in the background behind the scenes, to bring about the realization of truth and the reformation of the world. Such empty space (emptiness) and actual reality (the temporal) express the true Buddha way—that is, the dialectical dynamic of the bodhisattva way of duality in nonduality, and nonduality in duality.

A verse in chapter 15 says:

> They have learned the bodhisattva way well,
> And are untainted by worldly things,
> Just as the lotus flower in the water
> Emerges from the earth.[72]

In other words, they emerged from the earth like a lotus flower untainted by water, coming together in the here and now, untainted by worldly things. Here the bodhisattva way is explained through the symbolism of the lotus. That is, the idea that the lotus flower can only grow in muddy water, but also blossom there into a beautiful flower, is applied to the image of the bodhisattva. Moreover, it is taken from the title of the Lotus Sutra.

The lotus flower has been admired in India from ancient times, and was included in the Vedas and Upanishads as an object of religious admiration resembling the pure human spirit. It was also adopted in Buddhism and used with various meanings. But as we have seen, it seems to have been used mostly to symbolize bodhisattva practice in the early days of Mahayana Buddhism. The Vimalakirti Sutra, for example, says, "One is untainted by worldly things, just like the lotus flower, and is always able to enter the practice of emptiness and tranquility."[73] On the other hand, it also says that those who remain in a state of emptiness and willful nonaction[74] will not blossom into Buddha-dharma flowers and cannot become buddhas, and it criticizes such people for using the lotus symbol. Further, this sutra uses the metaphor "the lotus does not grow in highlands, but blossoms in muddy swamps," and says, "Only living beings in the mud of passions can rise to pursue Buddha-dharma."[75]

Chapter 16, "The Lifetime of the Tathagata," as it has been traditionally understood, reveals the eternal life of Shakyamuni Buddha. But the occasion for doing this was provided by a question raised in the previous chapter: How could the innumerable bodhisattvas who have emerged from below the earth have been taught and led to the Buddha way over the short span of the Buddha's life? The answer is given that the innumerable bodhisattvas have been authentic disciples of Shakyamuni Buddha. That is, in view of the fact that Shakyamuni Buddha only recently became awakened and became a buddha, how could he have so many disciples? Chapter 16 reveals that in reality Shakyamuni Buddha became a buddha an infinitely long time ago, thus an infinite amount of time has passed since he became Buddha. In this way we can see that the advocacy of the Buddha's universality is related to bodhisattvas.

The important thing to notice in chapter 16 is the way in which the Buddha's everlasting life is revealed. The text says:

> Thus, since I became Buddha, a very long time has passed, a lifetime of innumerable countless eons of constantly living here and never entering extinction. The time that I have devoted to walking the bodhisattva way is not finished even now, but will be twice as many eons as have already passed.[76]

This means that the eternal life of the Buddha is shown through infinite, never-ending bodhisattva practice. The everlasting or eternal life is realized by endlessly doing bodhisattva practice in this actual world.

Chapters 17 and 18 say that those who devote themselves to the truth of the one vehicle and the everlasting life, and make an effort to practice in this world, will be admired for their merit. And chapter 20 tells the story of the bodhisattva Never Disrespectful,[77] who serves as a model of the bodhisattva way. Despite various persecutions at the end of the eon, he did not lose hope that people would become buddhas in the future through practicing the bodhisattva way. He never disrespected anyone, but trusted all because of their buddha nature, repeatedly showing respect to everyone he met. Generally speaking, trust and reverence toward human beings are involved. In this way the chapter provides a typical model of the bodhisattva way.

In the spirit of the bodhisattva, and as a kind of model case of the bodhisattva way, the bodhisattvas who welled up out of the earth in chapter 15 are entrusted with the truth and encouraged with praise to embody it and put it into practice in the future. The words of chapter 21 were very meaningful and encouraging to Nichiren, and it is said that Dogen passed away while reciting passages from this chapter.

In chapter 22, the Dharma is entrusted to all others. Thus, the entrustment in chapter 21 was later called a "special entrustment," because it was directed only toward the bodhisattvas, such as Superior Practice Bodhisattva, who had welled up from the earth. The entrustment of chapter 22 was called the "general entrustment," because it is directed to all others. Those who are entrusted with the Dharma swear to fulfill the mission of the Buddha.

Thus, the entrustment of the Buddha's mission to bodhisattvas is completed and the stupa of Abundant Treasures Buddha, which had been suspended in the air, returned to where it originally came from, the assembled embodiment buddhas of Shakyamuni returned to their respective lands, and the bodhisattvas returned to this actual saha world—generally a reiteration of the significance of being born into this world. This is how the curtain falls on the second group of chapters.

Moreover, just a glance at chapters 10–22 shows us that bodhisattvas play an important role and are the main focus of these chapters. So we can say that the purpose of the second group of chapters, in contrast with the first, was to edify the bodhisattvas and to emphasize the bodhisattva way. The first group of chapters—the early part of the Lotus Sutra—claims that the truth of emptiness, positively understood, is the unifying truth of the cosmos. The second group establishes a picture of a unified world or cosmic reality based on this. There is then a need to explain a way of life based on this truth, or how to put this truth into actual practice. The second group of chapters was developed for this purpose.

The main part of the Lotus Sutra boils down to just this. Chapter 25 later grew to be so highly valued that it became an independent sutra, but it is supplementary to the distinctive character of the sutra as a whole. The chapters from 23 on were later added from the perspective that they guided the formation of the original text.

Chinese Translations and Sanskrit Manuscripts of the Lotus Sutra

According to records, there seem to have been many translations, both partial and complete, of the Lotus Sutra into Chinese. It has been said that there are six complete translations, three extant and three lost. We cannot trust that statement just as it is, but there are three extant Chinese translations: the ten volume, twenty-seven chapter, True Dharma Flower Sutra[78] translated by Dharmaraksha[79] in 286 CE; the seven volume, twenty-seven chapter (later eight volume, twenty-eight chapter) Wonderful Dharma Lotus Flower Sutra[80] translated by Kumarajiva[81] in 406 CE; and the seven volume, twenty-seven chapter, Appended Wonderful Dharma Lotus Flower Sutra,[82] which was a revision of Kumarajiva's translation by Jnanagupta and Dharmagupta[83] in 601–2 CE.

Dharmaraksha's translation is chronologically the earliest. However this does not necessarily mean that the Sanskrit version on which it was based was the earliest Sanskrit version. Since all of the Sanskrit originals of Chinese translations are lost, we cannot determine which was the oldest. Kumarajiva's is the most beautiful translation, and it has been the most used up to now. Manuscripts of Sanskrit texts have recently been discovered in Nepal, Kashmir, and Central Asia, under the auspices of a British man, B. H. Hodgson (1800–94). While living in Nepal as a government minister in the first half of the nineteenth century, Hodgson collected Sanskrit versions of Buddhist sutras, the Lotus Sutra being one among them. Many additional copies of Sanskrit manuscripts of the Lotus Sutra have been discovered since then.

These recently discovered manuscripts are roughly categorized into two groups: those from Nepal and those from Central Asia. The copies from Nepal are more apt to be complete, whereas many of those from Central Asia are fragmentary. Experts generally think that those from Nepal were copied during or after the eleventh century, and those from Central Asia were copied earlier than that. Among the latter group there is a hand-copied version (the Petrovsky manuscript) thought to be from the seventh or eighth century. More recently, a new minority view has arisen according to which several of the copies from Central Asia are later than those from Nepal.

The manuscript discovered in 1931 at Gilgit in Kashmir, which closely resembles the Nepalese versions, is believed to have been hand-copied in the fifth or sixth century, making it the oldest existing copy of this Buddhist sutra. Three quarters of the whole work have been found. The script style is cursive, which is typical of Gupta writing.

From 1908 to 1912, H. Kern, an Indian and Buddhist studies scholar of the Netherlands, and Bunyu Nanjo[84] of Japan published the Sanskrit text of the Lotus Sutra in Devangari script.[85] They revised their edition in accord with various copies in the Nepalese family, including the Central Asian Petrovsky manuscript, and others. Unrai Wogihara and Katsuya Tsuchida further revised their edition and published it in Roman script in 1934–35.[86] Kern produced an English translation based on the Sanskrit text mentioned above, and published it as *Saddharma-Puṇḍarika or The Lotus of the True Law* in 1884.[87] E. Burnouf, the French philologist and oriental studies scholar, made a translation of the Lotus Sutra into French from manuscripts given to him by Hodgson and published it in Paris in 1852.[88]

In addition to these, Surendrabodhi and Nanam Yeshe De made a Tibetan translation of the Lotus Sutra entitled *The Mahayana Sutra Entitled "The White Lotus Flower of the True Dharma"* at the end of the eigth and beginning of the ninth centuries. Ekai Kawaguchi translated this Tibetan version, with references to Sanskrit texts, into Japanese, and published it in 1924 as *A Translation from the Storehouse of Sanskrit Sutras: The Sutra of the White Flower of the Wonderful Dharma*.[89] Bunyu Nanjo and Hokei Izumi[90] also made a Japanese translation from Sanskrit texts, which they published in 1913 as *A New Comparative Translation of the Lotus Sutra from Sanskrit and Chinese*.[91] Kyosui Oka's *Lotus Sutra: A Japanese Translation from the Sanskrit* was published in 1924.[92] Since then a number of newer translations into Japanese have been published.

In addition to these, the Lotus Sutra has been translated into various languages from Sanskrit, Chinese, and Tibetan texts and is very widely respected.[93] Faith in the Lotus Sutra has been especially strong in China and Japan. Systematic teachings, worldviews, and philosophies of life based on the Lotus Sutra have been developed in those countries. It has been applied to political ideas and has had such an influence on literature that there has developed a Lotus Sutra literary genre.

II

Ideas of
the Lotus Sutra

3

Three Major Teachings in the Lotus Sutra

Appraisals of Lotus Ideas

EVALUATIONS OF THE Lotus Sutra have traditionally run to the two extremes. In this respect, too, the sutra is indeed a wonder. First of all, one of the most severe criticisms of the sutra is the idea that it has no content. In chapter 25 of *Emerging from Meditation*, Nakamoto Tominaga comments that "the Lotus Sutra praises the Buddha from beginning to end but does not have any real sutra teaching at all, and therefore should not have been called a sutra teaching from the beginning." Moreover, "the whole of the Lotus Sutra is nothing but words of praise."[94] In sum, the Lotus Sutra is nothing but words of praise either for the Buddha or for itself, teaches nothing like a doctrine, and therefore cannot properly be regarded as a sutra. In his book *Nakedness*,[95] Tenyu Hattori comments similarly on the Lotus Sutra, saying, "It is only a big story in the sky," meaning that it is only a big, empty, work of fantasy.

Atsutane Hirata, who abused Buddhism in vulgar and crude ways, ridiculed the Lotus Sutra in the third volume of his *Laughter Following Meditation*, saying, "The Sutra of the Lotus Flower of the Wonderful Dharma in eight fascicles and twenty-eight chapters is truly only snake oil without any really substantial medicine in it at all. If someone gets mad at me for saying this, I intend to tell him to show me the real medicine." This criticism that the Lotus Sutra is merely snake oil devoid of content later became famous and highly regarded, and the theory that the Lotus Sutra has no real content, represented by Hirata, has since become quite common.

Actually, if one only glances through the Lotus Sutra one may get the impression that it is nothing but snake oil without real substance. We can find something like doctrines in the first half, but they are not analytical and no detailed theory is developed from them. The second half of the sutra vigorously teaches faith in the Lotus Sutra. The Lotus Sutra does praise only itself, to put it bluntly. Nor does the Lotus Sutra say what kind of thing it itself is. So it is not unreasonable that the above criticisms arose.

But it is not the case that there has been no defense against such criticism. Tiantai Zhiyi already rejected such criticism in early times, saying that if the Lotus Sutra "does not discuss all kinds of Mahayana and Small Vehicle forms of meditation, the ten powers, fearlessness, and various standards, it is because these things have already been taught in prior sutras. It discusses fundamental principles of the Tathagata's teachings, but not the fine details."[96] In other words, in previous sutras the various detailed teachings and definitions are fully worked out, while the Lotus Sutra, generalizing upon them, aims to illuminate the fundamental and ultimate principles of Buddhism. Therefore, it does not discuss minute details of doctrine. In this sense, Tiantai Zhiyi calls the Lotus Sutra "genetic and essential," "the great cause," "the ultimate essence," "the essential structure of the teachings," "the Buddha's device for saving people," and so forth.

According to Tiantai Zhiyi, the Small Vehicle treatises and such teach many things in detail, making it appear at first glance as if these were the whole content of Buddhism, while in fact they are nothing more than a complex analytical philosophy that is subordinate to the synthetic philosophy found in works such as the Lotus Sutra. Citing these ideas of Tiantai Zhiyi, Nakamoto Tominaga once praised him, saying, "He should be regarded as one who has read the Lotus Sutra well." But in the end, Tominaga was not persuaded by Tiantai Zhiyi's way of understanding, concluding, "In reality he missed the mark."[97]

Another criticism of the Lotus Sutra is that it is merely a vulgar work meant to attract stupid men and women. This is what Tenyu Hattori said. For example, in chapters 18 and 25 and elsewhere, the sutra preaches about the benefits to be gained in this life as a result of faith in the sutra, such as the elimination of suffering and having good fortune. "This is just inferior, shallow stuff, best laughed at, for alluring stupid men and women. It's too inferior and shallow to think about," he said. "Its purpose is wholly to attract stupid lay people." Atsutane Hirata followed Hattori in this vein, remarking that chapter 25 had been highly valued for a long time, "becoming a separate sutra which ordinary Japanese people know as the Kannon Sutra," but which "only serves to attract stupid lay men and women because it is utterly clumsy."[98]

There are many places in the section of the Lotus Sutra that is considered to have come third historically that emphasize the benefits to be obtained in this life, such as the wonderful powers of faith, overcoming suffering, and having good fortune. And generally speaking, in later times devotion to the Lotus Sutra became mainstream as a result of these chapters. This is why such criticisms arose. As we have already seen, the third part of the sutra was added in order to respond to the magical and esoteric Buddhist and folk religions of India. It adds to and supplements the earlier parts of the sutra and, if taken in a positive way, can be its applied part. It is not appropriate to characterize the whole sutra in that way by emphasizing the third part, though historically admiration for the Lotus Sutra in China and Japan generally rested on that part. So, in one sense, we can understand why there were such criticisms.

Some contemporary Buddhist scholars view the Lotus Sutra as exclusive, contentious, and sometimes even combative. This can be regarded as another of the criticisms of the Lotus Sutra. Evidence for it being exclusive is found, for example, in the incident of the "departure of the five thousand" in the second chapter, in which five thousand people who did not understand the Buddha's teaching got up from their seats and left, and the Buddha did not stop them but called them the dregs of the assembly. Such scholars regard all of the Mahayana sutras as negative toward the Small Vehicle to some extent, but none as extremely so as the Lotus Sutra.

They also suspect that the extreme practices of martyrdom and self-sacrifice found in chapter 13 are examples of something created by a distinct social group that was exclusive, closed, and estranged from the general society. From this they try to prove the exclusivity of the Lotus Sutra. And they relate to this what they see as the exclusivity and contentiousness of Nichiren or his followers.

There are additional criticisms, but we have discussed the main ones. The interesting thing is that there were also evaluations completely to the contrary. That is, there were those who praised the Lotus Sutra for establishing the supreme and absolute unifying truth (the Wonderful Dharma of One Vehicle), for elucidating the ultimate reality of this universe (the reality of all things), and for integrating various ideas. Just as the Lotus Sutra refers to itself as "great impartial wisdom,"⁹⁹ followers of the Small Vehicle, who had been detested because they were never to become buddhas, are acknowledged by the Lotus Sutra as future buddhas under the unifying and integrating truth of the impartial one vehicle. In this respect the Lotus Sutra was seen as being the opposite of exclusive, namely inclusive and abundantly tolerant.

In India people highly praised this propensity for universal impartiality and the theory that one could become a buddha through the two Small Vehicle vehicles. This is taken up in various treatises. For example, the *Great Wisdom Discourse*, a commentary on the Large Perfection of Wisdom Sutra attributed to Nagarjuna, cites every chapter of the Lotus Sutra and sees the Lotus Sutra as being superior to the Large Perfection of Wisdom Sutra with regard to teaching becoming a buddha in the future for the followers of the two Small Vehicles. Moreover, various treatises of the fourth and fifth centuries, such as Ken'i's *Introduction to the Mahayana*¹⁰⁰ and Vasubandhu's *Commentary on the Lotus Sutra,* say the same thing. According to Vasubandhu, in particular, the Lotus Sutra teaches three equalities—the equality of truth (the equality of vehicles), the equality of worlds (the equality of societies), and the equality of existence (the equality of beings)—and explains the ten kinds of highest meaning.

What's more, the fourth century Great Final Nirvana Sutra emphasizes the ideas that all living things will become buddhas and that there is an eternal and universal existence (the everlasting existence of the Dharmakaya)—two ideas that are said to have come from the Lotus Sutra's ideas of the impartial one vehicle and of the Eternal Buddha. The Great Final Nirvana Sutra itself is certainly related to the Lotus Sutra. The treatises mentioned above discussed ideas such as the Eternal Buddha or the theory of the everlasting existence of the dharmakaya, using them to prove the profundity of the Lotus Sutra.

Some modern Japanese scholars, pointing to its teachings of the impartial one vehicle and of becoming buddhas through the two Small Vehicles, also hold the Lotus Sutra in high regard, seeing it as having the most richly tolerant and accommodating spirit among the sutras. They say that the idea of accommodation can be found throughout the Lotus Sutra. Tenyu Hattori, who lavishes praise on the Lotus Sutra for this, says, "On the whole, the Lotus Sutra is inclusive. This inclusiveness is comprehensively generous, giving it the dignity of a king."

In China, the Lotus Sutra was characterized as the teaching that unifies all good, meaning that all good ideas are brought together and unified in the Lotus Sutra. Inheriting this tradition, Tiantai Zhiyi created a single great philosophy with the Lotus Sutra as its nucleus. It is no exaggeration to say that Zhiyi achieved a unification and systematization of Buddhist thought for the first time. He made use of various sutras and treatises by taking as his central idea that the Lotus Sutra itself is a synthesis of broad and profound thought. He called the inclusiveness of the sutra "opening and integrating,"[101] and made it the key concept in his systematization of a philosophy of synthesis.[102]

Some of the modern scholars discussed earlier, who were critical of the Lotus Sutra, did not recognize the value of Tiantai doctrine and were extremely critical of it, saying such things as, "It is based entirely on ignorance and misunderstanding," and "It is unreasonable, to begin with, that the Lotus Sutra, which was originally popular and fanatic, is being dressed up as doctrine. In fact Tiantai doctrine has had almost no influence on general thought in China and Japan." But this critic contradicts historical fact and badly misunderstands the true situation. Tiantai doctrine has had great influence on the doctrines and practices of various other sects, such as the Huayan (Japanese: Kegon), Pure Land, Ch'an (Japanese: Zen), and others. At one time, it was even like their underlying foundation. There is no question that it influenced and was absorbed in general thinking.

In Japan, for example, Shikibu Murasaki's *Tale of Genji* is closely related to the Lotus Sutra and Tendai doctrine, to the extent that a theory of the unity of Genji and Tendai appeared in the latter part of the Heian period. The number of fascicles of *The Tale of Genji* is the same as the number of fascicles of the three great books of Tendai Zhiyi. Thus the idea developed that *The Tale of Genji* is Tendai doctrine put into the form of a novel. Of course, there were also some who opposed such a theory. In *A Little Jeweled Comb*, an interpretation of *The Tale of Genji*, Norinaga Motoori (1730–1801) says, "I do not believe it was Shikibu Murasaki's intention to get approval from Tendai, join the Tendai sect, and write everything from a Tendai perspective. Though this idea was intended as praise for her, it goes against her own intentions." Motoori thought that the penetrating thing about *The Tale of Genji* was that it is filled with the human feeling of *mono no aware*, the feeling of the transiency of nature. In contrast, he thought that there was something severe in Buddhism that denied human feelings and transcended human life, and that it was, accordingly, a mistake to see *The Tale of Genji* from a Buddhist perspective. "The way of the Buddha is especially a way of abandoning *mono no aware*. More strict than Confucianism, it wants to distance itself from all human sympathy."[103]

Motoori approved of pre-Buddhist Japan and for that reason wanted to forcibly remove all hint of Buddhism from Japanese culture and literature. One can detect this kind of prejudice in his interpretation and critique of *The Tale of Genji*. Yet we can also see keen insight in his identification of *mono no aware* as a distinguishing feature of *The Tale of Genji*. While Motoori declared this kind of intention to remove Buddhist influence, in fact we seem to have Japanese assimilation and acceptance of Buddhist ideas. At least it is a fact that Tendai Lotus thought had a great deal of influence on *The Tale of Genji*.

When it comes to medieval Japan, we can see the influence of Tendai Lotus thought on the poetic theory of Shunzei Fujiwara (1114–1204) and his son Teika (1162–1241). A new wave of yugen poetry arose centered around their thought, and in his *Poetic Style Through the Ages*,[104] Shunzei often uses terms from the Lotus Sutra and from Tendai meditation in recognition of the fact that they emphasized the depths of waka poetry.

Tendai Lotus thought also greatly influenced Shinto theory during the Middle Ages. Eventually, at the end of the Muromachi period, Kanetomo Yoshida[105] (1435–1511) brought this influence to fruition as monotheistic Shinto.[106] This development is notable for being the first time that a theory of native Japanese thought was developed. Here, Tendai doctrine—especially the Tendai idea of original enlightenment that was developing at the time—greatly influenced this monotheistic Shinto. The Tendai idea of original enlightenment, which we will discuss later, reached the final stage of its philosophical development at the end of the Heian period and during the Muromachi period. Its influence on the various Buddhist sects and on trends in literature and art is beyond our comprehension.

Dogen (1200–53), the founder of Japanese Soto Zen, in writing his multi-volume work *Treasury of the True Dharma Eye,* quoted from the Lotus Sutra more than from any other sutra, making his work seem as if it were an interpretation of the Lotus Sutra. We know that the Lotus Sutra played a very important role in the development of Dogen's profound philosophy. Hakuin Ekaku[107] (1685–1768), who revived Rinzai Zen in early modern times and founded the present Rinzai school, read the Lotus Sutra every day when he was forty-two. One night, when reading chapter 3, "A Parable," he suddenly awakened and began devoting himself to spreading the Dharma. He said this himself in writings, such as his letter in reply to Lord Nabeshima.[108]

When it comes to modern times, there are also people who have been profoundly moved by the Lotus Sutra, Tendai philosophy, and Nichiren's thought and have based their view of life on them. We will discuss this in more detail later. In any case, we must insist that it is an historical fact that the Lotus Sutra and Tendai doctrine have been very influential in Japan— both within Buddhism and more generally—since they were brought from China down to modern times.

The Unifying Truth of the Universe— The Wonderful Dharma of One Vehicle

When we look at the Lotus Sutra in light of its final form, we can see the merit of the traditional division of the sutra into two halves between chapters fourteen and fifteen. Daosheng (355–434),[109] a disciple of Kumarajiva who participated in the translation of sutras, made this division for the first time. Soon after the translation of the Lotus Sutra was finished, he wrote a commentary on it—the first in China, or at least the first that we still have.[110]

Daosheng divided the Lotus Sutra into two parts, according to the teachings of cause and effect. That is, the section from chapters 1 through 14 he defined as that which "explicates the three causes and makes them one cause," and the section from chapters 15 through 21 he defined as that which "speaks of three effects and makes them one effect." In addition, the remaining chapters were interpreted as that which "makes three kinds of people equal and makes them one." Here, "three" signifies the three vehicles and "one" signifies the one vehicle.[111]

On the other hand, Daosheng established the idea of four kinds of Dharma wheel: the good and pure Dharma wheel (general religious thought), the Dharma wheel of skillful means (Buddhist *upaya*), the true Dharma wheel (true Buddhist thought), and the perfect Dharma wheel (ultimate Buddhist thought). The true Dharma wheel is what reveals the truth of the one vehicle, while the perfect Dharma wheel reveals the everlasting life (the Buddha). The teaching of cause, chapters 1–14, corresponds to the true Dharma wheel, while the teaching of effect, chapters 15–21, corresponds to the perfect wheel of Dharma. The remaining chapters are the dissemination or applied part of the sutra.

Fayun[112] (467–529) of Guangzhai Temple, who wrote *Principles of the Lotus Sutra*[113] following Daosheng's interpretation, defined the teaching of cause as "opening up three and revealing one" and the teaching of the effect as "opening up the near and revealing the far"—the latter being extended to the final chapter. "Opening up three and revealing one" means that the three kinds of vehicle that lead toward the truth—shravaka, pratyekabuddha, and bodhisattva vehicles—are unified as one vehicle. And "opening up the near and revealing the far" means that the historical Shakyamuni Buddha is revealed as being in truth the eternal Buddha.

Tiantai Zhiyi inherited the idea of the two teachings of cause and effect but replaced them with the teachings of the "provisional" and the "original." Moreover, he developed a detailed account of the construction of the Lotus Sutra into an introductory part, a central core, and an applied part. We can see this in the first half of the first volume of his *Textual Commentary on the Lotus Sutra* and as outlined in the chart below. In addition, it was around the time of Tiantai Zhiyi that the Devadatta chapter was inserted as chapter 12 of the Sutra and all subsequent chapters renumbered accordingly, the former chapter 12, "Encouragement to Uphold the Sutra," becoming chapter 13.

Tiantai Zhiyi's reason for dividing the Lotus Sutra into two parts between chapters fourteen and fifteen was that he saw the first half, centering around

Tiantai Zhiyi's Divisions of the Lotus Sutra

One Sutra, Three Stages	Chapter	Two Halves, Six Stages
Introduction	1	Introduction
Central Core	2–9	Central Core
	10–14	Application
	15	Introduction
	15–17	Central Core
Application	17–28	Application

chapter 2, as revealing the integrating truth of the cosmos (the Wonderful Dharma of One Vehicle), while the second half revealed the eternal personal life (the original eternal Buddha). Following this division, I would now like to review in outline these chapters one by one. Since most commentators have used Kumarajiva's translation, so will I.

Chapter 1, "Introduction," is a kind of prologue. The scene is set on Mt. Gridhrakuta (Eagle Peak) in the city of Rajagriha, the capital of Magadha in north-central India. When the curtain rises, we see Shakyamuni Buddha on the mountain, accompanied by a vast assembly, including his first disciples and all sorts of beings from every level of society. Having first preached the vast and innumerable meanings of the truth, he goes into deep meditation. Then the Buddha emits a ray of light from the white tuft between his eyebrows, lighting up everything in the entire cosmos. This is a prelude to delivering the supreme and ultimate teaching. Recollecting that such a thing had happened many, many ages ago, the whole assembly is eager to hear the Buddha's sermon.

In chapter 2, "Skillful Means," the Buddha arises from his meditation to explain first the truth about all things in the cosmos (the ultimate reality of all things). According to Kumarajiva's translation, every thing happens and functions in ten ways, such that everything has characteristics, a nature, an embodiment, powers, actions, causes, conditions, effects, rewards and retributions, and a complete fundamental coherence.

"Characteristics" means an outward aspect. "Nature" means inner character. "Embodiment" means the outward and the inner characters together. "Powers" means potential. "Actions" means actual acts. "Causes" are the direct causes that give rise to and move things. "Conditions" are the indirect causes that facilitate direct causes. "Effects" are the results produced by causes and conditions. "Rewards and retributions" are the facts that issue from the effects. "Complete fundamental coherence" means the coherent interrelationship of all of these.

Since "such a/an"[114] precedes each of these in translation, they have been called the "ten suchnesses." They have been highly regarded since ancient times as the aspects of existing things and events. The ten suchnesses are the truth that supports and underlies every kind of thing, making them coherent "dharmas." Or, put the other way around, the concrete truth that supports all kinds of things is the ten suchnesses. It is the reality of all things.

When we understand the categories of the ten suchnesses, we will see that nothing is independent or unchanging (the doctrines that nothing has a permanent self and of emptiness), but everything is interdependent, being related to others as it arises and changes (the doctrines of impermanence and of interdependent origination). The Lotus Sutra finds the unifying truth of the cosmos in the interrelating of all things, all dharmas, under the ten suchnesses. This unifying truth of the cosmos was called "the Wonderful Dharma of One Vehicle."

After explaining the reality of all things found in the ten suchnesses, the second chapter introduces this unifying truth of the cosmos. As it is the supreme, absolute truth, it is called the true Dharma or the wonderful Dharma (*saddharma*). In other words, as the vehicle that integrates all dharmas and things as the highest way, it is called the one vehicle or the one Buddha-Vehicle. It has also been called the Buddha's supreme and ultimate teaching (the primordial teaching).

Up to this point, the Buddha had taught various teachings and truths, such as the two or three vehicles, according to the level and capacity of the audience. Now it was time to explain the supreme and absolute truth that would synthesize and unify those various teachings. This is the ultimate purpose of the Buddha. "The tathagatas teach the Dharma for the sake of all living beings only by means of the One Buddha-Vehicle. They have no other vehicles—no second or third vehicle." The buddhas of the past and of the future "through an innumerable variety of skillful means, causal explanations, parables and other kinds of expression, have preached the Dharma for the sake of living beings. These teachings have all been for the sake of the One Buddha-Vehicle. . . ."115

> In all the buddha-lands in the ten directions
> There is only the Dharma of one vehicle,
> Not a second or a third . . . 116

> * * * * *

> By using the power of skillful means
> They demonstrate various paths.
> But they are all really for the sake of the Buddha-Vehicle.117

Later, terms such as "skillful means of three vehicles and the truth of one vehicle" came from such passages. Furthermore, the reason chapter 2 was named "Skillful Means"118 was that the main theme of the chapter is the explication of the "skillful means of three vehicles and the truth of one vehicle."

On this point we need to look at the historical development of Buddhist thought, which is in fact mentioned in chapter 2. During and after Shakyamuni Buddha's time there were two types of Buddhists: shravakas—disciples who sought awakening through hearing the Buddha's teachings—and pratyekabuddhas or self-enlightened ones—ascetics who sought awakening by individually observing the appearance of causes and conditions and the coming into existence and passing away of human life and nature. As shown in detail earlier, seeing the transiency and emptiness of life, many of them fell into nihilism and ended up losing the meaningfulness of life.

Then, at about the time of the beginning of the current era in the Western calendar, a group, called "bodhisattvas," appeared who devoted themselves to practicing the truth in the actual world. They created a Buddhist reform movement, in which they criticized the earlier two vehicles as being lesser vehicles (*hinayana*), while calling themselves the Great Vehicle (*mahayana*). They were especially harsh on the nihilism of the followers of the two vehicles in which the possibility of becoming a buddha had been lost.

The transiency and emptiness of life that Shakyamuni Buddha taught does not end with such nihilism but leads to the infinite and absolute world that is like empty space. Through realization of such a world, the great joy and meaning of life is reborn by liberating those who suffer from clinging to the ups and downs of life. Those who try to be witnesses to this truth are the bodhisattvas of Mahayana Buddhism.

Mahayana bodhisattvas first tried to elucidate the principle of emptiness and then incorporated it in sutras, the first of which was the Great Perfection of Wisdom Sutra. Beyond that, they tried to express emptiness positively, as an empty place where the unifying truth (the Wonderful Dharma of One Vehicle) can be seen, in other words, in the Lotus Sutra.

The establishment of this unifying truth also teaches us to see the world and life not from a narrow, partial, or temporally limited perspective but with a holistic, eternal vision. This truth can save modern people from being increasingly maddened and captivated by the fragmentation of whole systems. In a word, it creates an image of a holistic cosmos, an integrating and unifying view of the world and of life. As I will later show, this is the reason for the emergence of people who had acquired this kind of view of the world and human life: they had been touched by the unifying truth and integrating cosmic reality (the reality of all things) revealed in the heart of chapter 2. The Tiantai theory of "three thousand worlds in one moment of experience" was the harbinger of this way of thinking.

Moreover, the second chapter teaches that the nihilistic followers of the two vehicles, which it criticizes for not being able to become buddhas, are once again awakened to the unifying truth of the one vehicle and are reborn to the possibility of becoming buddhas like everyone else. This teaching, known as "the ability of the two vehicles to lead to becoming a buddha," became one of the outstanding characteristics of the Lotus Sutra, which generally speaking, places emphasis on the equality of all people and all things under the unifying truth. From chapter 3 on, various parables and narratives tell the story of how, through this unifying truth, followers of the two vehicles can be saved from the abyss of nihilism, how all human beings can be saved from clinging to the world of illusion, and how they are, moreover, guaranteed to become buddhas in the future. Later generations often used these parables as literary material.

The famous parable of the three vehicles and the burning house appears in chapter 3. The burning house represents human life, and the three vehicles—the goat, deer, and ox carts—represent the shravaka, pratyekabuddha, and bodhisattva ways. Without realizing that they are in the midst of and being consumed by the fire of life, human beings seek life's pleasures. In order to save them the Buddha tries to get them to get out of the burning house by offering them things appropriate to their abilities and liking (i.e., the three vehicles, teachings of skillful means). When they go outside, all alike are given great white ox-carts (the One Buddha-Vehicle). The following passage is famous and often recited in Japanese:

> The threefold world is not safe,
> Just as a burning house
> Full of all kinds of suffering
> Is much to be feared.

> Always there is the suffering of
> Birth, old age, disease, and death.
> They are like flames
> Raging ceaselessly.

> The Tathagata is already free
> From the burning house of the threefold world.
> He lives in tranquil peace,
> As in the safety of a forest or field.

> Now, this threefold world
> Is all my domain,
> And the living beings in it
> Are all my children.

But now this place
Is filled with all kinds of dreadful troubles,
From which I alone
Can save and protect them.[119]

Nichiren showed with this passage, which he greatly admired, that Shakyamuni Buddha is our lord, teacher, and parent ("the Three Beneficial Virtues").

In chapter 4, "Faith and Understanding," is found the parable of the rich man and the poor son, in which a rich man corresponds to the Buddha, and the poor son indicates the nihilism of Small Vehicle Buddhists. The great rich man had only one son, who had run away from home while still young. In extreme poverty, the son became a wandering beggar. The son, having become used to a life of begging, accidentally returned to a place in front of his father's house, but fled in fear of the magnificent mansion. The father then thought about what to do and hired him to clean latrines. Since it suited him, he did this kind of work in his father's house for twenty years. As the son gradually became used to this work, the father disclosed that he was his father and gave his incomparable wealth to him. When he realized this, the son was overjoyed.

This is a story about how very difficult it is for someone who has sunk to the bottom of nihilism to get out. At the same time it is a story of how, being skillfully led to the Wonderful Dharma of the One Vehicle, one can finally return to life. Furthermore, the mental state of the poor son—of the nihilistic followers of the Small Vehicle—is described in Kumarajiva's translation as follows:

> The World-honored One has been teaching the Dharma for a long time, and all the while we have been sitting in our places, weary in body and mindful only of emptiness, of formlessness, and of non-action. Neither the enjoyments nor divine powers of the bodhisattva-dharma—purifying buddha-lands and saving living beings—appealed to us.[120]

Freely translated, the same words in verse are:

Even if we had heard
About purifying buddha-lands
Or teaching and transforming living beings,
We did not aspire to do them.

Why? Because all things are empty and tranquil
Without coming to be, without extinction,
And without existence. Being without faith,
This is how we thought.

Chapter 5 has the simile of the plants. From a great cloud, rain falls equally on all, and from the great earth, blessings come equally to all. But just as various kinds of plants grow luxuriantly, the truth that the Buddha discovered and the things the Buddha taught, though one and the same for all, are different according to differences in listeners' abilities to understand. Regarding "three plants and two trees," "small plants" refers to the common thinking of human and heavenly beings, "medium-sized plants" to the thought of the two Small Vehicle vehicles, "large plants" to the thought of Mahayana bodhisattvas. "Small trees" refers to bodhisattvas who benefit only themselves, and "large trees" to bodhisattvas who benefit others.

This chapter emphasizes the oneness of the truth taught by the Buddha and the equality of his compassion. "The Dharma taught by the Tathagata is one and the same for all."[121] "The Buddha's unbiased teaching is like the single flavor of the rain."[122] "I look upon all, without exception, as equal, without distinction, or any thought of love or hate."[123] "Constantly, for the sake of all, I teach the Dharma equally."[124] Further, we find the following kind of expression: "Those who have not yet been saved will be saved; those who have not been set free will be set free; those who have had no rest will have rest; those who have not yet obtained nirvana will obtain nirvana. I understand both the present world and the worlds to come as they really are. I am one who knows all, one who sees all, one who knows the Way, one who opens the Way, one who teaches the Way."[125]

In chapter 6, "Assurance of Becoming a Buddha," the Buddha reassures the four great disciples (the shravakas of chapter 4) and five hundred other disciples that they will become buddhas in the future. The basis of this assurance is given in chapter 7. Here we find the parable of the treasure and the fantastic (or temporary) castle-city. The way to the truth is steep; people become discouraged along the way. Then the Buddha provides a temporary truth (the three vehicles) according to the ability of people and lets them rest there. When they are rested, the Buddha encourages them to pursue ultimate truth (the one vehicle).

This is the truth taught in the parable of the fantastic castle-city. Temporary truth is likened to a castle-city, and ultimate truth to a great treasure. The four noble truths are taught to shravakas as temporary truths, the law of twelve causes to pratyekabuddhas, and the practice of the six transcendental practices (*paramitas*) to bodhisattvas. Finally, they are all led to and awakened by the one vehicle—that is, by ultimate truth.

This "opening, showing, becoming enlightened, and entering" is also in chapter 2. Tiantai Zhiyi thought very highly of these words and theorized about them in several ways. Many Buddhist sects very highly respect the following words from chapter 7 as a vow, and chant them in Buddhist services.

> May these blessings
> Extend to all,
> That we with all the living
> Together attain the Buddha way.

The number of disciples who are assured of becoming buddhas in the future increases from five hundred to twelve hundred in chapter 8, where we also find the parable of the priceless jewel in the lining of a robe. A good friend told a penniless man that he had sewn a priceless jewel into the lining of his robe when he was drunk. This story is thus about recovery. The poor, drunken man is likened to disciples who had fallen into nihilism, the friend is the Buddha, and the jewel in the lining of the robe is their hidden possibility of becoming buddhas through acts of compassion (bodhisattva practice). We are taught that:

> Keeping their bodhisattva actions
> As inward secrets,

Outwardly
They appear as shravakas.

Thus the disciples who had fallen into a nihilistic way of life, including the solitary practitioners, were all revived by the Buddha's call. And they received assurance of becoming buddhas in the future. Chapter 9, which follows, is a summary of this.

Within this group of disciples were some who still had room to learn and some who were regarded as having no further need of study. Those who attained the stage of not having anything more to learn were called *arhats*. An arhat is a saint who deserves people's respect and reverence. Essentially, it was another term for the Buddha, used with a positive connotation. But after the rise of Mahayana Buddhism it was often used as a pejorative term for Small Vehicle Buddhists who had become nihilistic because they thought there was nothing more they needed to learn in life.

Such Small Vehicle Buddhists can be regarded as being of two kinds: direct disciples of the Buddha and solitary practitioners. Later, in addition to "Small Vehicle," it came to be called "the two vehicles." Be that as it may, what we see in chapter 9 is that all the Small Vehicle Buddhists, both shravakas and pratyekabuddhas, are assured of becoming buddhas in the future whether they are in need of further learning or not. With this the chapter ends. As the text says, "Then the two thousand people in training and no longer in training, hearing the Buddha's assurance, were ecstatic with joy."[126] The significance of this is that the form of the Lotus Sutra is such that, through this chapter, the Buddha speaks to his direct disciples, the shravakas. "Two thousand" is just a round number and can be taken to mean all followers of the Small Vehicle.

Chapter 10 teaches the unifying and ultimate cosmic truth, i.e., the Wonderful Dharma of One Vehicle. What had previously been revealed should now be put into practice in this actual world, and thus made concrete. This idea emphasizes the bodhisattva way. Bodhisattvas, who have thus far played only modest roles in the sutra, now come to the fore as the main actors.

In the section of this book on the history of the formation of the Lotus Sutra, we saw that we can regard chapters 10–22 as a group that emphasizes bodhisattva practice. We have also examined the contents of these chapters, and therefore we do not need to do so again. Here I only want to introduce some interpretation, parables, and phrases from this part of the sutra that have traditionally received attention. I also want to touch on the "Devadatta" chapter (12), which, as mentioned earlier, was inserted into the sutra around the time of Tiantai Zhiyi.

The so-called "three principles for spreading the sutra" and the parable of the thirsty man have traditionally been highly valued and given prominence in the tenth chapter. The three principles are three tracks for practicing the truth in the real world: compassion, patience, and the ability to see the emptiness of all things. These three are represented in chapter 10 by the room, the robe, and the seat of the Tathagata. The Lotus Sutra says:

> To enter the room of the Tathagata is to have great compassion
> for all living beings. To wear the robe of the Tathagata is to be
> gentle and patient. To sit on the seat of the Tathagata is to con-
> template the emptiness of all things.[127]

In the parable of the thirsty man, a man goes to a high flat area to dig for water to quench his thirst. When he finds the soil dry, he knows that the water is still far away, so he continues to dig. When he strikes damp soil, he knows that water is near. In the same way, when a bodhisattva makes an effort to practice, he can be sure that he is approaching truth. In this way, the sutra unflaggingly promotes bodhisattva practice.

In addition to this parable, there are several other notable teachings in chapter 10, which have already been touched on. Nichiren was especially attracted to the term "apostle" or "emissary" of the Tathagata, which appears there. Influenced by this term, Nichiren used the phrase "follower of the Lotus Sutra." The Lotus Sutra says, in connection to the phrase "emissaries of the Tathagata," that those who devote themselves to embodying the truth in this world even a little are people who have been sent from the pure world of the Buddha to be born in this world because they have compassion for people. This suggests a meaning or purpose for being born in this world. Nichiren was able to gain courage and meaning for living from this kind of phrase, despite having to bear much suffering.

In chapter 11, a jeweled stupa rises up out of the ground and hangs in the air. Shakyamuni Buddha shifts his seat from Mt. Gridhrakuta to the jeweled stupa in the air. Thus the scene changes from the meeting place on Mt. Gridhrakuta to the meeting place in the air. After chapter 22, the setting returns to Mt. Gridhrakuta. This has been called the "three meetings in two settings."

The especially notable things in chapter 11 include the rising up out of the ground of a jeweled stupa, the two buddhas sitting side-by-side, the gathering together of Shakyamuni Buddha's embodiment or representative buddhas, and the one universal buddha-land. I have already introduced these in the section on the history of the formation of the Lotus Sutra. This chapter also teaches and explains the so-called "six difficult and nine easy practices" concerning the proclamation of the Lotus Sutra. Further, the verses at the end of the chapter, from "This sutra is so difficult to embrace . . ." up to the last phrase, ". . . should receive offerings from all human and heavenly beings,"[128] are known as "the phrases of difficulty in embracing the sutra," or the "jeweled stupa verses." Even now people continue to recite them frequently.

Chapter 12 tells about the future becoming a buddha of Devadatta, the extremely evil one who rebelled against Shakyamuni, and the sudden awakening of an eight-year-old dragon girl. This chapter has been revered since ancient times as an expression of the awakening of evil people and women. While the esoteric Shingon school often uses the term "becoming a buddha in one's present body,"[129] it was first used when Zhanran, the sixth patriarch of the Chinese Tiantai school, interpreted chapter 12.[130] The chapter may have been inserted into the Lotus Sutra later[131] and does not form a natural part of the narrative line of the sutra as a whole. Yet, for the reason mentioned above, it is still revered and recited.

Chapter 13, the martyrdom chapter, tells of the consciousness-raising of bodhisattvas, in which they become envoys of the Buddha by pledging to take the Buddha's orders seriously as they undergo suffering by working for the realization of truth. These bodhisattvas promised:

> Though many ignorant people
> Will curse and abuse us
> Or attack us with swords and sticks,
> We will endure it all.

* * * * *

In an evil age of a muddied eon,
Full of dreadful things,
Evil spirits will take possession of others
To curse, abuse, and insult us.

But, revering and trusting in the Buddha,
We will wear an armor of patient endurance.

* * * * *

We will cherish neither our bodies nor our lives,
But care only for the unexcelled way.

* * * * *

Repeatedly we will be driven out
And exiled far from stupas and monasteries.
Remembering the Buddha's orders,
We will endure all such evils.

* * * * *

We will go there and teach the Dharma
Entrusted to us by the Buddha.

We are emissaries of the World-Honored One.
Facing multitudes without fear,
We will teach the Dharma well.[132]

This section was very moving to Nichiren, who read it as something to be taken to heart and put into practice.

Chapter 14 teaches that bodhisattvas who devote themselves to the social application of the truth should develop the habit of self-reflection. Whereas the previous chapter has the so-called stern, "break and subdue" method of conversion, this chapter has the mild, "embrace and accept" method of leading others. It discusses ways of admonishing oneself and controlling one's behavior, speech, attitudes, and will. These are called the four kinds of trouble-free or "safe and easy" practice.

The chapter also advises against such things as getting too close to kings, ministers, other high officials, and the like, smiling or laughing or having a covetous attitude while preaching to women, and putting others down or abusing them with talk about their likes and dislikes or good and bad points. It gives detailed instructions on such things as not forgetting to be compassionate and respectful to others, or praying that all will be saved. Even though we are in this world, the emptiness of all things should not be forgotten. And bodhisattvas should dwell "as peacefully and unmoved as Mount Sumeru."[133]

Another interesting thing is the fact that, in chapter 4 of the *Commentary on the Lotus Sutra* attributed to Prince Shotoku (574–622), commenting on the phrase "always preferring meditation (*zazen*) in a quiet place, he should improve and quiet his mind,"[134] the author questions how bodhisattvas can find the time to spread the sutra in the world if they always like to meditate in secluded mountains. So he read the passage in a different way, such that it meant that one should not get close to or be friendly with Small Vehicle Buddhists who like meditation. In other words, he interpreted it as saying "Do not get close or friendly with Small Vehicle zen masters who always like to be doing meditation." When the author of that commentary read this text in this way or simply ignored it, he would mention it, saying such things as "I interpret it a little differently" or "I don't need this now." Strangely enough, this was an impetus for the advent of practical-minded Japanese thought. At least it provides good material for understanding the Japanese adoption of Buddhism.

Chapter 14 also contains the parable of the jewel in the topknot. A powerful king rewards his soldiers for their achievements. The precious jewel in the topknot of his hair is the only thing he does not give to anyone, reserving it for a soldier of especially great merit. Just as the Buddha, who is king of the truth, has preached the Dharma in various ways, the Lotus Sutra is reserved for those who will practice the bodhisattva way in the future.

This is traditionally where the first half of the sutra, the teaching of cause or of the historical Buddha, comes to an end. The second half, the teaching of effect, or of origin, begins with the next chapter.

Everlasting Personal Life—The Everlasting Original Buddha

In chapter 15, some of the bodhisattvas who had come from other worlds offer to teach the sutra in this saha world for Shakyamuni Buddha. But he rejects their offer, saying that there are already millions and millions of bodhisattvas in the saha world who will follow him in spreading the Dharma. As soon as he says this, innumerable bodhisattvas emerge from below the earth and come before the Buddha. They are referred to as "the bodhisattvas who emerged from below the earth." They have four leaders—Superior Practice, Unlimited Practice, Pure Practice, and Firm Practice.[135]

The people who see this are surprised, and ask Shakyamuni Buddha where these bodhisattvas had come from and why. Shakyamuni reveals that they lived in the empty sky under the saha world and, unlike those from other worlds, are his own authentic disciples and Dharma children. Pondering this, the people have trouble believing that Shakyamuni, who had become awakened not so long ago, could have so many disciples who were so proficient. It would be like a twenty-five-year-old man claiming to have a one-hundred-year-old son!

This is the gist of chapter 15. The most important thing in it is that the chapter praises this saha world—that is, it praises those who make great efforts while enduring suffering in this actual human world. They are the true disciples of the Buddha. The chapter is critical of those immediate disciples of the Buddha who preach the bodhisattva practice of enduring suffering in this world while separating themselves completely from the actual world.

Also, we should not neglect the idea that these bodhisattvas live in the empty sky under the saha world. I have already pointed out that the term "empty sky" also means "unlimited," and is used in a way parallel to "emptiness." That is to say, living in the emptiness in the saha world means to be in the midst of the swirl of the world of desire, without being dragged down by it, constantly maintaining a stance of unattached freedom.

Concerning this way of being a bodhisattva, the last verse section of chapter 15 includes the phrase, ". . . and [they] are untainted by worldly things, just as the lotus flower in the water emerges from the earth."[136] The lotus grows only in muddy water, yet its beautiful flowers bloom without being tainted by the muddy water. Thus, a bodhisattva should live in this actual world without being tainted by the mud of the world, like beautiful flowers blooming with truth.

Chapter 16, responding to the perplexity of people in chapter 15, explains that Shakyamuni Buddha is really the Everlasting Original Buddha using the metaphor of the five hundred dust particles worth of eons. Suppose someone ground into fine dust five hundred thousand billions of myriads (*nayuta*) of countless (*asamkhya*) three-thousand great thousandfold worlds, and just one particle of this dust was deposited on every five hundred thousand billions of myriads of innumerable lands until all of the dust was exhausted, and then all of these worlds, those with a particle of dust and those without, were ground into dust. If one particle of dust is regarded as equivalent to an eon, the period of time equivalent to all of the dust particles is nowhere near as long as it has been since Shakyamuni became a buddha.[137]

An eon is a long time. A *nayuta* is usually taken to mean one hundred billion. The word *asamkhya* means an uncountable number. And "three-thousand great thousandfold worlds" refers to the result of adding together three kinds of thousandfold world—small, medium, and large. It is said that a small thousandfold world corresponds to the solar system, a medium one to the galaxy, and a large one to a nebula. In chapter 7, there is a story in which one of these three-thousand great thousandfold worlds is ground into particles of dust and one particle is deposited on every thousandth world. It is called "the parable of the three thousand dust particles of eons." In short, the story emphasizes the Buddha's eternal life by means of these similes of very large numbers.

> Thus, since I became Buddha a very long time has passed, a lifetime of innumerable countless eons of constantly living here and never entering extinction.[138]

Some readers may get the impression from this that this everlasting, imperishable Shakyamuni Buddha is the personal God of monotheism. Hendrik Kern, who edited the Sanskrit text of the Lotus Sutra and translated it into English, had such an impression. His research led him to conclude that the

Lotus Sutra is similar to the Bhagavad Gita and had been influenced by it. The Bhagavad Gita is presumably from about first century India. Its ancient religious poetry is full of songs of praise for a monotheistic and personal God. Most Indian people, down to the present, have come to love to recite its beautiful and passionate verses.

In the introduction to his translation of the Lotus Sutra into English, Kern discusses similarities between the Lotus Sutra and the Bhagavad Gita, even comparing similar expressions in them. For example, Kern points to verses from chapter 16 of the Lotus Sutra, such as:

> [I am] the father of the world, the Self-born, the Healer, the Protector of all creatures. Knowing them to be perverted, infatuated, and ignorant I teach final rest, myself not being at rest.

> Then I assemble the crowd of disciples and show myself here on the Gridhrakuta . . . and I have not left this Gridhrakuta for other abodes.[139]

These he says are similar to verses from the Bhagavad Gita, such as:

> Although I am indeed unborn and imperishable, although I am lord of the creatures, I do resort to nature, which is mine, and take on birth by my own wizardry.

> I am the father of this world. [They] find in me their savior from the ocean that is the run-around of deaths.[140]

And he cites words from chapter 5, such as:

> I am inexorable, bear no love nor hatred towards any one, and proclaim the law to all creatures without distinction, to the one as well as the other.[141]

And he compares them with the phrase from the Bhagavad Gita:

> I am equitable to all creatures, no one is hateful to me or dear.[142]

In chapter 21, the Lotus Sutra tells us that Shakyamuni Buddha and Abundant Treasures Buddha reveal their divine powers by extending their tongues up to the Brahma heaven, and emitting from them countless rays of light, from each of which innumerable bodhisattvas emerge, illuminating the worlds of the ten directions:[143]

> Inconceivable is the power to promote the weal of the world possessed by those who, firmly established in transcendent knowledge, by means of their unlimited sight display their magic faculty in order to gladden all living beings on earth.

> They extend their tongue over the whole world, darting thousands of beams to the astonishment of those to whom this effect of magic is displayed and who are making for supreme enlightenment.[144]

Kern maintains that this has the same content as the following, from Bhagavad Gita 11:30:

> You are greedily licking your lips to devour
> These worlds entire with your flickering mouths:
> Your dreadful flames are filling with fire,
> And burn to its ends this universe.[145]

Some other scholars tend to understand such descriptions of the Buddha in the context of the solar myth or the veneration of the sun.

As we have seen, Kern compares the Lotus Sutra with the Bhagavad Gita, maintaining that the Gita influenced the sutra. Yet there is reason to disagree with this. The Gita teaches a Creator and a cosmic creation, while in the Lotus Sutra the Everlasting Buddha is not regarded as the Creator, and there is no term equivalent to "creation." Furthermore, the Bhagavad Gita emphasizes passionate and fanatical devotion (*bhakti*) to God, while we cannot find the idea of passionate and fanatical devotion to God anywhere in the Lotus Sutra.

Faith is emphasized throughout the Lotus Sutra. The Sanskrit terms used for it are *shraddha*[146] (faith) and *adhimukti*[147] (faith and understanding). In addition, *prasada*[148] (pure faith) is used once or twice. None of these words means the kind of absolute devotion to an absolute person indicated by the term *bhakti*. They signify entering the Buddha way, reforming oneself, setting one's resolve, and purifying one's heart. With this kind of preparation one can devote oneself to the discipline, grow in wisdom, and become awakened.

This conception of faith has consistently underlain Buddhism. There is a place in the first chapter of Nagarjuna's *Great Wisdom Discourse*, that says, "Entering the great sea of Buddha-dharma is accomplished with the power of faith and attained by the power of wisdom." The Lotus Sutra also keeps this basic principle. Chapter 17, for example, while emphasizing a single moment of faith (*shraddha*) or faith and understanding (*adhimukti*) says that they go beyond five of the six transcendental practices, but adds "except the perfection of wisdom." That is, among the six practices for becoming awakened, only the last one, wisdom, or *prajna*, is put above faith.

In Christianity, where the absolute God of monotheism was affirmed, the relation between reason and faith became a big issue, and arguments developed around three positions—having faith in order to know, knowing in order to have faith, and having faith although it is irrational. In Buddhism, such serious arguments never arose, because the conception of God found in monotheism does not exist in Buddhism. In other words, the Everlasting Buddha of chapter 16 of the Lotus Sutra is essentially different from the One God, the supreme deity commonly seen in India, and from the monotheistic deity of Christianity and other religions. That being the case, how did the idea of an Everlasting Buddha come to be? And what is the Everlasting Buddha? In order to clarify this, we will need to review the theory of the Buddha in Buddhism.

To begin with, in comparison with his disciples and followers, Shakyamuni is the awakened one (the *buddha*), who became awakened to the truth (*Dharma*) or reality of the universe. When he died, he left these words, "Let the truth be your teacher." However, the disciples and faithful always heard the truth through the great personality of Shakyamuni. For them, the truth was the Dharma of the Buddha himself as well as the Dharma he taught. Thus, after Shakyamuni died his disciples and followers began to cherish his memory, paid respect to his remains, and placed his bones in stupas where they were venerated.

On the other hand, some could not be satisfied with relics and came to question what he was now that he had died. Then the idea arose that Shakyamuni's historical body—the *rupakaya*[149] or living body—had perished and become one with the everlasting truth, while Shakyamuni's original body— the *dharmakaya*[150] or truth-body—had never perished. At the same time, Shakyamuni was thought to be truly everlasting—the everlasting truth, the dharmakaya—which appeared in the world in a transformed or appearance body in order to save people. Accordingly, Shakyamuni's fleshly body, as the transformed or appearance body, could not be conceived of as one that is born and dies like those of ordinary people. So his death was regarded as something he had chosen himself.

Thus the theory of Buddha-bodies began to develop. It continued down to the fourth century as a theory of two bodies, but in Vasubandhu's *Commentary on the Lotus Sutra* we can see the idea of three bodies—a *nirmanakaya* or response body, [151] a truth body, and a *sambhogakaya* or reward body.[152] The response-body is concrete and has a beginning and an end. The truth-body is universal in the sense of having no beginning and no end, but is abstract. The reward-body is both universal and concrete. That is why it is called "the body of virtue produced by practice." The theory of Buddha-bodies was more or less completed with the development of the theory of the three bodies.

However, as we can see in the theory of the Buddha-body above, even though Shakyamuni Buddha is everlasting in the immortal truth, since this is abstract, it does not satisfy people's hearts. So Buddhists sought a concrete buddha, and views of the Buddha developed side by side with the theory of the Buddha-bodies. First, a buddha to replace Shakyamuni Buddha was created. Shakyamuni Buddha is everlasting in truth, yet we can no longer see his concrete appearance. Thus the expectation arose that the Buddha would appear sometime in the distant future in a concrete body different than that of Shakyamuni. This is the idea of a future buddha. Maitreya is that buddha. It is believed that he lives in his Tushita heaven, from which in 5,670,000,000 years he will appear on earth, become the buddha replacing Shakyamuni, and save people.

Before the idea of a future buddha arose, there was the idea of past buddhas. Out of deep reverence for the great Shakyamuni Buddha, people imagined that he had been a buddha in past ages, and that in turn there had been various kinds of past buddhas. In short, at the time of his death, what "Shakyamuni Buddha" meant was only the individual Shakyamuni, but after that, various kinds of past and future buddhas were imagined.

After the idea of the future buddha arose, the idea of buddhas of the afterlife and buddhas of other lands came into being. In other words, the idea that those who have already lived when Maitreya appears will not be able to meet him raised a problem, giving rise to the idea that, even in the present, one can meet a buddha in another land. This is the idea of buddhas of the afterlife and other lands. Amitabha in the Western Land and Akshobhya Buddha in the Eastern Land, both of whom can be found in chapter 7 of the Lotus Sutra, are good examples of this. As time went by, people came to think that since they could not wait for Maitreya to appear, they would be reborn directly into his Tushita heaven.

Faith in Maitreya as the future buddha and in Amitabha as the buddha of the afterlife have flourished down to the present. Such faith became especially strong during times when people felt they were living in the last days of history. Most new religious movements in modern Japan included such faith in Maitreya and looked to the coming of Maitreya's reign. Generally, faith in Maitreya and in Amitabha were practiced side by side to such an extent that two popular, ecstatic dances—the *Nembutsu* dance (related to Amitabha) and the Maitreya dance—simultaneously emerged.

Moreover, chapter 25 of the Lotus Sutra emphasizes the protective power of the bodhisattva Avalokiteshvara.[153] Thus, faith in Avalokiteshvara also flourished—a faith that pursued worldly benefits. During China's Song dynasty (from the second half of the tenth to the second half of the thirteenth century), Confucianism, Taoism, and Buddhism were often embraced together. Buddhism blended the worship of Amitabha, Maitreya, Avalokiteshvara, and others, in addition to Ch'an practice. In particular, faith in Amitabha, which guaranteed rebirth in a land of peace and bliss in the next world, and faith in Kwan-yin (Avalokiteshvara), which prevented calamities and gave happiness in this world, thrived as assurances. The proverb "In every house a Kwan-yin, everywhere the teachings of Amitabha" was born. The Buddhism of that time was transmitted to Vietnam, where it remains to this day.

With the development of the idea of buddhas of the afterlife and of other lands, the idea also developed that the Buddha is now somewhere in this world. This is called the idea of the present buddha. Further, breaking through the boundaries of the directions, the idea appeared that buddhas exist in all of the ten directions. From the time of the formation of the Mahayana Nirvana Sutra and the like, which is thought to have occurred in the fourth century, we see a theory of the Buddha's immanence, which claims that the Buddha is immanent in every person as a buddha-nature or *tathagatagarbha*.

Thus, as the theory of the bodies of the Buddha and the view of the Buddha became intertwined, people sought a great variety of buddhas. The Lotus Sutra and the everlasting Shakyamuni Buddha of chapter 16 were produced as part of this process. Originally "the Buddha" meant Shakyamuni. Thus the everlasting Shakyamuni Buddha of chapter 16 was to return the notion of "the Buddha" to Shakyamuni, and in the process to unify the various buddhas under Shakyamuni Buddha. This was the primary purpose of the theory of the everlasting Shakyamuni Buddha—to return "the Buddha" to Shakyamuni.

Second, the actual Shakyamuni is the living form of eternal life and the manifestation of a transhistorical Shakyamuni in history. Accordingly, even if that manifestation disappears, Shakyamuni does not. He exists eternally, beyond ordinary ways of viewing or thinking about being and nonbeing. Those who go beyond such ways of viewing or thinking can grasp this. This is the second meaning of the theory of everlasting Shakyamuni Buddha. In brief, the transhistorical Shakyamuni Buddha and the historical Shakyamuni Buddha are united.

It is already implicit in chapter 11 that Shakyamuni both exists eternally and unifies the bodies of the various buddhas. The Treasure Stupa hangs in the air, with the two buddhas—Abundant Treasures and Shakyamuni—sitting in it side by side. Shakyamuni going to the seat in the stupa in the air represents the infinite spatial extension of his world. Since Abundant Treasures Buddha is a previous form of Shakyamuni Buddha, their sitting side by side represents the infinite temporal extension of Shakyamuni's existence. The various buddhas of the ten directions are embodiments of Shakyamuni, which indicates that the true body of Shakyamuni is manifested everywhere. The return to Shakyamuni of all of these embodiments of him as he enters the stupa indicates that the worlds of the ten directions are unified into one buddha-land. This, too, is intended to reveal that Shakyamuni Buddha is a unifying Buddha.

Chapter 16 finally completely reveals that Shakyamuni is really the Everlasting Original Buddha. Shakyamuni himself emphasizes this, saying that the everlasting Shakyamuni goes beyond the ways of thinking about and viewing things used by ordinary people, who cling to being and nonbeing. The sutra says, "The Tathagata has insight into the threefold world as it really is. For him there is no birth or death, neither retreat from nor emergence into the world, no transmigration or extinction, neither being nor nonbeing, neither existence nor nonexistence, neither sameness nor difference, and neither deception nor nondeception. He does not see the threefold world through the eyes of an ordinary person."[154]

Thus, those who are deluded by inverted or perverse ways of thinking cannot see Shakyamuni:

> Perverse living beings fail to see me
> Even though I am close.[155]

It is before those who are upright and gentle, and have put attachment to desire behind them, that Shakyamuni appears:

> And when the living have become faithful,
> Honest and upright and gentle,
>
> * * * * *
>
> Then, together with the assembly of monks
> I appear on Holy Eagle Peak.[156]

In other words, those who are free from attachment to such things as being and nonbeing are able to see the Buddha.

It can be said that the Lotus Sutra turned the search for a concrete buddha back to Shakyamuni and attempted to see the eternal in the concrete Shakyamuni Buddha. Prior to the Lotus Sutra, even though the truthbody behind Shakyamuni was eternal, Buddhists would have thought of the actual and concrete Shakyamuni Buddha as being extinguished. This is why they sought a concrete buddha to replace Shakyamuni. In contrast, the Lotus Sutra maintains that the actual and concrete Shakyamuni is in reality a version of the eternal. That is, the eternity of Shakyamuni Buddha that is emphasized is not a truth-body behind him, but the concrete and actual Shakyamuni himself. In other words, the concrete, historical, actual Shakyamuni is the living embodiment of eternal life. His death or extinction, on the other hand, was just an expression of a convenient, temporary device.

The Buddha appears to be invisible in the teaching of chapter 16, in order to open the eyes of those who have narrow ways of thinking about being and nonbeing, and such. This is his so-called extinction. Those who have their eyes open know that the concrete and actual Shakyamuni Buddha exists eternally. This matter is summarized in lines of beautiful poetry in the verses at the end of the chapter. Kumarajiva's translation of them begins with a phrase that has been lovingly recited from ancient times: "Since I became a buddha ..."

We had to wait until after the Lotus Sutra for a logically coherent theory of the bodies of the Buddha. But on the whole the Lotus Sutra is consistent in terms of the conception of the Buddha. The idea of the Everlasting Original Buddha found in chapter 16 was conceived quite differently from the monotheism of the Bhagavad Gita or of Christianity and the like, as discussed above. To put it bluntly, what this means is that the Everlasting Original Buddha of the Lotus Sutra was never given the attribute of being a Creator. He was given various honorific titles indicating that he is supreme and absolute, but not a word was said about creation.

In Christianity, the one and only absolute and personal God must be the Creator of the universe. Such monotheism is seen as the ultimate form of religion, and Christianity is seen as typifying such monotheism. It was from such a point of view that some said that the existence of Amida Buddha or the everlasting Shakyamuni Buddha showed that Buddhism was close to Christianity as the ultimate religion. We can still hear such ideas, but we must say that this is looking at the matter from a Christian point of view.

The interesting thing is that when Christianity came to Japan in premodern times, there was deep controversy with Buddhists precisely about this matter, and controversies about other fundamental issues developed beyond this. Such things are truly remarkable, as this kind of Buddhist-Christian debate about profound intellectual issues could not be found in other countries. On the Buddhist side, followers of the Lotus Sutra were fiercely critical of Christianity.

Yet, even if we allow that the object of worship is the Buddha, within Buddhism—which began as faith in the truth—the question was raised as to why worship a person at all. This has become an important research topic within the science of the study of religions, which applauds value-neutral, objective research. It is a matter that Buddhists should objectively reexamine.

Though I have already devoted several pages to explaining chapter 16, I want to discuss this chapter's parable of the good physician before moving to the next chapter. In this story, a father—a physician—cannot convince his children, whose minds have been warped by poison, to take an antidote. So he leaves some medicine for them, disappears, and then sends someone to tell his children that he is dead. Hearing this, a deep longing for the father arises in the hearts of the children, bringing them to take the medicine. As a result they are cured and their eyes opened. Hearing that they had recovered, the father reappears. The children in the parable correspond to lost and wandering beings, and the father corresponds to the Everlasting Original Buddha. The father's disappearance is comparable to that of the Everlasting Original Buddha, who has a kind of temporary extinction in order to correct the people's hearts and minds and open their eyes.

The parables of the three carriages in chapter 3, and of the lost son in chapter 4, the simile of the rain and plants in chapter 5, the parables of the magic city in chapter 7, the jewel in the hem in chapter 8, the jewel in the topknot in chapter 14, and this parable of the physician's sons in chapter 17 are called the seven parables of the Lotus Sutra and have been highly valued from ancient times.

Chapters 17–19 praise the merits (or blessings) of those who devote themselves to the Lotus Sutra's teachings about practice in the world and of dedication to the One Vehicle of the Wonderful Dharma and the Everlasting Original Buddha. Chapter 17 teaches the theory of practice that later came to be summarized as the "four forms and five kinds of faith." The "four forms of faith" are: (1) having even a single moment of faith in and understanding of the sutra, (2) understanding its meaning, (3) being devoted to preaching it to others, and (4) continuing to maintain and develop profound faith and understanding. These were taken to have been taught during Shakyamuni Buddha's lifetime and thus were called "four forms of faith for the present." They involve developing a view of life and of the world in which one whole-heartedly accepts that the life of the Buddha is everlasting. In other words, it is to have faith instantly, understand its meaning, widely teach it to others, and in the process deepen one's own faith.

The "five kinds of faith" include: (1) rejoicing from receiving the Lotus Sutra, (2) reading and reciting it, (3) preaching it, (4) concurrently practicing the six transcendental practices, and (5) intensively following the six transcendental practices. These faith practices benefit those who devotedly put them into actual practice after Shakyamuni is gone, and thus they were called "the five kinds of faith following the extinction of the Buddha." They involve hearing the Lotus Sutra, rejoicing in and embracing it, reading and reciting it, teaching it to others and having them read it, and, at the same time, practicing the six transcendental practices—generosity, morality, patience, perseverance, concentration, and wisdom. Furthermore, one should be devoted to practice based on the six transcendental practices as the central focus of one's life.

The chapter emphasizes the idea that the blessings that come from practicing these four forms and five kinds of faith are innumerable and boundless, far superior to building temples or stupas. Fundamental among them are the faith and joy that arise from hearing of the eternal life of the Buddha and the ultimate truth. No discipline or practice can bear fruit without them. In this sense, what is being taught is that these four forms and five kinds of faith are superior to the five transcendental practices (excluding the transcendental practice of wisdom), the most important Mahayana teaching about practice.

The chapter teaches that when such faith and joy arise an absolute state is grasped then and there. This has already been taught in chapter 11. In that story, Shakyamuni climbs up to the stupa in the air and the buddhas of the ten directions are reunited with him, thereby connecting the worlds of the ten directions into one buddha-land. At that moment "this world instantly became pure, with lapis lazuli for earth, adorned by jeweled trees, and with cords of gold marking the boundaries of its eight divisions."[157] We find similar verses in chapter 16. Kumarajiva's translation of them is often recited, as they are regarded as beautiful:

> When the living witness the end of an eon,
> When everything is consumed in a great fire,
> This land of mine remains safe and tranquil,
> Always filled with human and heavenly beings.
>
> Its gardens and groves, halls and pavilions,
> Are adorned with all kinds of gems.
> Jeweled trees are full of flowers and fruit,
> And living beings freely enjoy themselves.
>
> Gods beat on heavenly drums,
> Always making various kinds of music.
> Mandarava blossoms rain down
> And are scattered over the Buddha and the great assembly.[158]

Translated freely, chapter 17 emphasizes ". . . this world—with its land of lapis lazuli smooth and level, its eight roads marked off with Jambunada gold and lined with jeweled trees . . ."[159] Tiantai Zhiyi absolutized this pure land as a world of ever tranquil light. And Nichiren, following the name given to it in the sutra, called it the pure land of Gridhrakuta, because that was the actual place where Shakyamuni preached.

Chapter 18 explains in detail the joy that is the first of the five kinds of faith in the previous chapter. Suppose someone rejoices upon hearing the sutra and passes it on to others, enabling them to pass it on with joy to still another person, until it has reached the fiftieth person. That joyous person's blessings will be far greater than those of someone who has donated many treasures or achieved the highest mental state of Small Vehicle Buddhism, that of the *arhat*. How much greater, it says, are the blessings of the initial person who hears the sutra and rejoices. That person's blessings are beyond comprehension. This has been called the joy of a fifty-person line of transmission.

Chapter 19 extols those who embrace, read, recite, explain, and copy the Lotus Sutra—that is, those who reap the merits of the five practices of a Dharma teacher. Their abilities, both physical and mental, are said to demonstrate excellence through purification of the six organs—the eyes, ears, nose, tongue, body, and mind. It teaches, for example, that they can see without limit to the edge of the infinite universe, hear all the sounds throughout the ten realms, from purgatory to the buddha-land, such as sorrows, grief, fears, sufferings, pleasures, joys, and so forth. To such a person, everything in the infinite universe is alive. Such a one has complete command over all things.

This means that by entering a life of religious faith one's previous life is dramatically transformed, the ordinary is broken through, such that extraordinary powers previously hidden may emerge. Generally speaking, this means that by observing the world extensively and objectively, and by deeply investigating the true nature of things, a self-reliant dynamism for facing the actual world will emerge. And this may lead to bringing truth to life in the actual world, freely making the best possible use of things as needed.

In chapter 2 is a passage that reads:

> The buddhas, the most honored of people,
> Know that nothing exists independently,
> And that buddha-seeds arise interdependently.
> This is why they teach the one vehicle.

> Things are part of the everlasting Dharma,
> And the character of the Dharma in the world endures forever.[160]

These verses have been used from ancient times to show respect for that part of the explanation of the mental organ that appears in chapter 19, where it says:

> And their many teachings will be in accord with the meanings,
> and never contrary to the true nature of reality. If they teach
> about some secular text, or speak about the political world or

about matters related to livelihood, in every case they will do so in accord with the true Dharma.[161]

Chapter 20 shows the actual practice of the truth—that is, it provides a model for bodhisattva practice. It is about bodhisattva Never Disrespectful, who endures all sorts of persecution during a time when the Dharma is in decline. Believing that all people will become buddhas through bodhisattva practice, he persists in never putting down or disrespecting anyone. Whenever he meets someone, he always calls out something like "Good people, I do not slight or make light of you. I can't slight or make light of you. Why? All of you walk in the bodhisattva way and should become all-wise, perfectly enlightened, worthy buddhas."[162] He was beaten with sticks, stoned and driven away, but responded with "I would not dare to disrespect you. Surely all of you are to become buddhas."[163] In this way he single-mindedly practiced respect for others.

Bodhisattva practice is an expression of love for all of humanity equally, rooted in infinite trust of human beings. Nichiren took the practice of never disrespecting and always revering others as a matter of positive and aggressive propagation[164] of the Dharma.

In chapter 21 we find the paradigm of bodhisattva practice and the expectation of the final entrustment of the mission to embody the truth to them. First, Shakyamuni Buddha reveals the ten kinds of divine power and praises the greatness of the truth of the Lotus Sutra. He tells bodhisattva Superior Practice and the other bodhisattvas:

> The divine powers of buddhas, as you have seen, are innumerable, unlimited, inconceivable. Even if for the sake of entrusting this sutra to others I were to use these divine powers to declare its blessings for innumerable, unlimited hundreds of thousands of billions of countless eons, I would be unable to exhaust them. In brief, all the teachings of the Tathagata, all the unhindered, divine powers of the Tathagata, the hidden core of the whole storehouse of the Tathagata, and all the profound matters of the Tathagata, are proclaimed, demonstrated, revealed, and preached in this sutra. Therefore, after the extinction of the Tathagata, you

should all wholeheartedly embrace, read and recite, explain and
copy, and practice it as you have been taught.[165]

Further, it teaches that wherever you are, if you revere the teachings of
the sutra and practice them, the Buddha will manifest in a state of absolute
and supreme happiness. That is:

> In any land, wherever anyone accepts and embraces, reads and
> recites, explains and copies, and practices it as taught, or wher-
> ever a volume of the sutra is kept, whether in a garden, or a
> woods, or under a tree, or in a monk's cell, or a layman's house,
> or a palace, or in a mountain valley or an open field, in all these
> places you should put up a tower and make offerings. Why? You
> should understand that all such places are places of the Way. They
> are where the buddhas attain supreme awakening; they are where
> the buddhas turn the Dharma wheel; they are where the buddhas
> reach complete nirvana.[166]

The tower in this quotation is not a stupa in which remains are kept, but a
caitya in which sutras are kept, signifying the reverent keeping of the teachings of the sutra. And the last Chinese word in the quotation, *bān nièpán,*[167]
is a phonetic translation of *pari-nivriti*, which, like *pari-nirvana*, signifies
the world of complete awakening or the state of supreme bliss.

When Dogen became seriously ill, he walked around in his room reciting
these words. He wrote them on a pillar, and finally named his monastery
room the "Lotus Sutra Hermitage."[168] When one walks through life vigorously, fully in accord with one's abilities, even if its ends are not yet complete, if a great, awakened letting-go arises, one can be satisfied. Dogen came
to such a realization through the words of this chapter.

Furthermore, the latter half of chapter 21 consists of verses with the same
idea. They have long been popularly and lovingly recited. The chapter closes
with these words:

> After the extinction of the Tathagata,
> Anyone who knows the sutras preached by the Buddha,

Their causes and conditions and proper order,
Will teach them truthfully in accord with their true meaning.

Just as the light of the sun and the moon
Can dispel darkness,
Such a person, working in the world,
Can dispel the gloom of living beings,

Leading innumerable bodhisattvas
Finally to dwell in the one vehicle.
Therefore, one who has wisdom,
Hearing of the blessings to be gained,

After my extinction
Should embrace this sutra.
Such a person will be determined to follow,
Without doubts, the Buddha way.[169]

From these verses Nichiren became aware of what it means to be born in the latter days, and of his own mission. And though his heart was crushed by suffering, he enthusiastically took up his mission once again. At that time, he developed his so-called "Five Categories of Teaching"—five things that have to be taken into account for disseminating the Dharma: the teaching, the hearers, the age, the country, and the sequence of propagation.

In chapter 21, the bodhisattvas, centering around Superior Practice Bodhisattva, are given the mission to propagate the Dharma (the "special entrustment"), and in chapter 22 this is extended to all the bodhisattvas (the "general entrustment"). Those so entrusted make vows to dedicate themselves to following the Buddha's orders[170] and to working to embody the truth. "We will respectfully do all that the World-Honored One has commanded. Please, World-Honored One, do not worry about that."[171] A very similar vow can be seen in chapter 13.

When the Buddha's entrustment orders were completed, the stage of the drama returned from the air to Mt. Gridhrakuta on the ground, and those who received the mission distributed themselves around the saha world. The main story line of the Lotus Sutra ends here. The remaining six chapters are supplemental, yet the merits and efficacy of faith are emphasized and taught in various distinct ways in them. Thus, these chapters came to be highly regarded among the people. Only the main points will be mentioned here.

Chapter 23 tells the story of a bodhisattva who burned his body and, in a later incarnation, burned his arms as offerings to the Buddha. The chapter praises the virtue of such actions. The term for burning one's body as an offering[172] comes from this story. The blessings of faith derived from this and the efficacy of such a faith are taught in this way:

> Just like a clear, cool pool, it can satisfy all who are thirsty. Like fire to someone who is cold, like clothing to someone naked, like a leader found by a group of merchants, like a mother found by her children, like a ferry found by passengers, like a doctor found by the sick, like a lamp found by people in the dark, like riches found by the poor, like a ruler found by the people, like a sea lane found by traders, and like a torch dispelling the darkness, this Dharma Flower Sutra can enable all the living to liberate themselves from all suffering, disease, and pain, loosening all the bonds of mortal life.[173]

And in the chapter we can find such words as:

> If anyone is sick, when they hear this sutra their sickness will quickly disappear and they will neither grow old nor die.[174]

We may think that faith gives a person strength and power to overcome life's difficulties and physical illnesses, and the words above may be quoted for this purpose. Yet in later times such words were taken literally, and so people developed faith in the Lotus Sutra for the purpose of receiving worldly benefits.

However, the main idea of chapter 23 ultimately has to do with transcending mortal life—that is, they have to do with "cutting the bonds of life and death" and "defeating the armies of life and death."

> ... blowing the conch of the Dharma and beating the drum of the great Dharma, save all living beings from the sea of old age, sickness, and death.[175]

On the other hand, while burning the body as an offering was meant to symbolize the faith of one who gives unstintingly of his life,[176] it was also taken literally. One can find examples in China and Japan in which this was actually put into practice. There often appear chapters on self-immolation in the biographies of eminent Chinese monks, and those biographies mention the fact of people offering their bodies. In Japan, stories and biographies from the late Heian period tell of many who died from burning their own bodies trying to reach the buddha-land. Stories that describe, for example, peeling off one's skin and portraying the Buddha on it, or cutting off a leg and making a buddha statue out of the bone, are thought to be exaggerations. We are not sure to what degree they are true. Yet these things probably did happen to some extent, considering that the authorities banned attempting to attain a birth in a buddha-land through such acts as self-immolation, drowning oneself, or donating oneself to animals (which means throwing away one's body in mountains or fields).

As we saw several years ago in Vietnam, people used such acts to call for the world to awaken, and as a powerful means of resisting the power of the existing regime. Yet, while we cannot help but feel that their purpose was lofty, it left an even stronger impression that such acts are abnormal and tragic. Some committed such acts for magical effect, or as a quick way to attain the peace and bliss of birth in the buddha-land, or as an expression of their ambition to achieve posterity. The occurrence of such evil things brought on the government ban. This was the situation in China and also in Japan, going back as far as the rules for priests and nuns that appeared in the Taiho Code.[177]

Chapter 24 uses the model of bodhisattva Wonderful Voice to describe the mental concentrations (*samadhi*) and divine powers of liberation that are acquired through faith. Here faith is meant to foster a kind of immovable and transcendent spirit drawn to involvement in the eddies of this changing world. The chapter emphasizes cultivating such an ability to be able to cope with this world as well as is possible.

Chapter 25, "The Universal Gateway of the Bodhisattva Regarder of the Cries of the World," attracted so much respect among people that it became an independent sutra. Here Avalokiteshvara personifies the illumination of the entire world, perceiving it and responding with saving help. According to this chapter, it is possible to be rescued from the seven dangers—fire, water, people-eating demons, swords, demons, torture, and robbery—by chanting the name of the bodhisattva. One can also remove the three poisons—greed, anger, and stupidity. And those wanting to have a baby boy or a baby girl will be able to by doing the same.

In order to save people, Avalokiteshvara transforms himself into thirty-three different bodies according to people's desires and capacity to understand—an act that symbolizes the bodhisattva's infinite compassion. In brief, "this bodhisattva can confer fearlessness on living beings." As one who confers fearlessness,[178] Avalokiteshvara Bodhisattva removes peoples' fears. That is, the purpose of this chapter is to encourage people to try to live their lives in faith without fear.

Chapter 26 teaches incantations (*dharani*) for the protection of the followers of the Lotus Sutra. The word dharani is translated into Japanese as "remembering all"[179] (for the power of maintaining everything in memory), as "ability to hold"[180] (for firmly keeping good teachings), and as "ability to block"[181] (for firmly insulating oneself from bad teachings). Dharani, regarded as having efficacious power, are a kind of incantation, and are products of esoteric Buddhist thought.

The name "Mother of Demon Children"[182] appears in this chapter. She swears to try to protect the followers of the Lotus Sutra. According to legend, she was originally a demon who snatched children and ate them,[183] but after being admonished by the Buddha was transformed into a deity who protected children. The appearance of the name in this chapter provided an opportunity for faith in Mother of Demon Children to become popular within the Nichiren school.

If anyone resists our incantations
And makes trouble for a Dharma preacher,
Their heads will split into seven pieces. . . .

* * * * *

Good, good, if you can protect those who receive and keep even
the name of the Dharma Flower Sutra, your blessings will be
immeasurable.[184]

People have often recited passages such as these. These phrases, the
dharani, and Mother of Demons were all used to promote a kind of faith
that is beneficial for combating calamity and inviting good fortune in this
world.

Chapter 27 tells a story about two princes who converted their father,
a non-Buddhist king, to faith in the Lotus Sutra. These words are often
quoted from it:

A buddha is as difficult to meet as an udumbara flower, or as a
one-eyed tortoise meeting the hole in a floating log.[185]

Chapter 28 teaches the four kinds of normative conduct appropriate to
the Lotus Sutra: securing the protection of the Buddha, planting roots of
goodness, joining a good congregation, and resolving to save all beings. It
then teaches in various ways the protection of followers of the Lotus Sutra
through the grace of the Bodhisattva Universal Sage (Samantabhadra),
which in turn became Universal Sage's vow to practice the faith.

The Lotus Sutra itself comes to an end here. Yet the Sutra of Contemplation of the Dharma Practice of Universal Sage Bodhisattva[186] (which is
in line with chapter 28 of the Lotus Sutra) immediately follows, and has
been taken as the concluding sutra of the Lotus Sutra, just as the Sutra of
Innumerable Meanings (in line with on the "innumerable meanings" found
in chapter 1) was placed at the beginning of the Lotus Sutra and regarded as
its opening sutra. The three sutras taken together are called "The Threefold
Lotus Sutra." The Contemplation of Universal Sage Sutra emphasizes the
vow of Universal Sage to practice the faith, or the repentance part of his

meditation on practice. The theory of reality repentance[187] found in this sutra especially has received much attention.

Reality repentance is the teaching that:

> The whole ocean of hindrances from past actions
> Arises from illusion.
> If you want to repent, you should sit upright
> And reflect on the true nature of things.
> All sins are like frost and dew.
> The sun of wisdom can dissipate them.[188]

Here the key point has to do with meditation on emptiness. In other words,

> What is sin? What is virtue? As the thought of self is itself empty, neither sin nor virtue is our master.[189]

It recommends that:

> You should recite the Great Vehicle
> And meditate on the emptiness and formlessness of things . . .[190]

The sutra itself calls this "repentance without sin."[191]

This "repentance without sin" was later misunderstood to mean that there is neither sin nor evil. But originally it was based on being captivated by sin or evil, and it advocates getting rid of such captivation through meditation on emptiness. Tiantai Zhiyi created the Lotus *samadhi* or meditation on the basis of this reality repentance.

Human Action in This World—The Bodhisattva Way

Since we have surveyed the Lotus Sutra according to the traditional view of its division into two parts, and have already seen that there are three parts to the sutra with regard to its historical formation, we need to look at one more part and describe its distinctive teachings. This part consists of chapters 10–22, which overlap both of the traditional two divisions. As we will look at this part from the point of view of historical formation, chapter 12, which may have been inserted later, will not be discussed here.

As we have seen in the section on the historical formation of the sutra, this part of the sutra was composed as one group in accord with a consistent intention: it was done to emphasize bodhisattva practice. Bodhisattva practice means human activity in the world, which is the characteristic idea that runs continually through this group of chapters, from the beginning to the end. We have already examined the original Sanskrit text, so there is no need to repeat that here. Yet I do want to review once more just the important parts related to the traditional division.

First of all, let us look at chapter 11. As mentioned before, in this chapter there is the sudden appearance of the Treasure Stupa, the two buddhas sitting side by side, the gathering together of the buddhas who are embodiments or representatives of Shakyamuni, the united buddha-land, the purification of the saha world, and so on. These things were traditionally understood to imply that Shakyamuni Buddha is the Everlasting Original Buddha, and were taken to herald chapter 16, "The Life of the Tathagata." But chapter 11 also teaches the propagation of bodhisattva practice, which is its ultimate purpose. We can see this in the following:

> Who is able to teach the Wonderful Dharma Flower Sutra everywhere throughout this world? Now indeed is the time. Before long the Tathagata will enter nirvana. So that it will last forever, the Buddha wants to entrust this Wonderful Dharma Flower Sutra to someone.[192]

Thus, it encourages actual bodhisattva practice in this world during the latter days and teaches the entrusting of the Dharma to such bodhisattvas.

Next, chapter 16 is traditionally understood as showing that Shakyamuni is the Everlasting Original Buddha, and from that point of view, is regarded as the core of the second half of the Lotus Sutra. Since it does maintain the eternal life of Shakyamuni, such an interpretation certainly seems reasonable, but it is important to notice how that eternal life is taught.

The inception of the revelation of the everlasting life of Shakyamuni Buddha is in chapter 15, where a question is raised about the countless bodhisattvas who emerged from the earth and were said to have been taught from the remote past by Shakyamuni. Here at its inception, the teaching of the eternity of Shakyamuni Buddha is already related to bodhisattvas.

> Thus, since I became Buddha a very long time has passed, a life-time of innumerable countless eons of constantly living here and never entering extinction. Good sons, from the beginning I have practiced the bodhisattva way, and that life is not yet finished....[193]

In short, unlimited, endless bodhisattva practice is used to demonstrate the eternal life of the Buddha.

What the sutra says here may at first give the impression that the conception of eternity is inconsistent. The story about the five hundred specks of dust does the same. Fayun (467–529),[194] one of the annotators of the Lotus Sutra, commented that eternity in the sutra is only an extension of time and space, not an eternal or absolute truth that breaks through the limits of time and space. Because he was seeking an eternal truth, Fayun adopted the Nirvana Sutra's teaching of the eternal life of the Buddha's Dharma-body.

But the idea of living forever, which seems to be inconsistent on first impression, is really one of the intellectually powerful and characteristic conceptions of the Lotus Sutra. It shows that eternal life becomes alive and vivid within unlimited bodhisattva practice amid the dynamic movement of history. From this point of view, we can see that the idea of the Everlasting Original Buddha of chapter 16 is qualitatively different from so-called traditional monotheism.

The idea of the Everlasting Original Buddha should be considered in light of the development of Buddhist thought. We can recognize that it was stimulated by the rise of a monotheistic trend that appeared in much of India around the first century. However, the influence of monotheism only stimulated it; it did not produce it. We can find nothing in the Lotus Sutra that indicates that the Buddha is the creator of the whole universe, nor is there any other theory of the origin and development of the universe or of the generation of everything in it at the hands of the Buddha.

Indian monotheism was different from the Christian kind of monotheism, which affirmed only one God. Indian monotheism selected one god as supreme among the many that it recognized. Max Müller (1823–1900), who did research on and published the Rig Veda, an ancient Indian religious text, and was editor of *The Sacred Books of the East*, called this kind of Indian monotheism "henotheism." And since the supreme god could change, he also termed it "kathenotheism" for religions in which one god at a time is supreme. Japan's idea of Amaterasu-omikami and other gods is typical of henotheism.

In brief, while we can make a distinction between monotheism and henotheism, either of them can have a Creator. To this day we can hardly find such an idea in Buddhism. The Lotus Sutra, too, as a product of Buddhism, excludes the idea of a Creator. On the other hand, Glasenapp and others thought that the words "unceasing bodhisattva practice" were a late addition to the Lotus Sutra. He maintained, in other words, that the sutra emphasizes the idea of a suffering savior, using its symbolically existing eternal being to reject such things as the creation or governance of the world—notions which contradict fundamental ideas of Buddhism.

The Everlasting Buddha is not a Creator but unceasingly engages in bodhisattva practice. Moreover, the sutra teaches that our becoming a buddha is substantially the same as it is for the Everlasting Original Buddha, but is expressed in different terms. For what purpose, then, does the sutra insist upon the idea of Everlasting Original Buddha? We can summarize it in the following three points:

1. It resolves views of the Buddha—in other words, its purpose is to bring together and make coherent the various buddhas. In this regard, we can say that whereas we find the unity of Dharma or truth in chapter 2, we find the unity of Buddha or the personal in chapter 16.
2. It shows that we can see the personal life of the Everlasting Original Buddha wherever there is unified truth—that is, it reveals that the unifying truth of the cosmos is not merely a matter of natural law, but that the eternal body of truth, which affects all life, is personal and dynamically alive.
3. It shows that the dynamism of eternal life can inspire us in the midst of religious practice within this life. This is why chapter

16 teaches that Shakyamuni Buddha is the Everlasting Original Buddha and that he has never ceased doing bodhisattva practice.

From the perspective of historical formation we can see chapters 10–22 as a group created in order to show that such inspiration can be found in the midst of ordinary life. This part of the sutra should be recognized as a kind of third division, in contrast with the traditional two-part division.

Nichiren was one who paid special attention to this part of the sutra. For this reason he insisted on the idea of "a third teaching," saying, "The teachings of Nichiren are the third teaching." Tiantai Zhiyi's idea of the third "doctrine" lies behind this. His "three kinds of doctrine" are (1) the inclusiveness or noninclusiveness of all kinds of people, (2) the universality or nonuniversality of transformation, and (3) closeness to or distance from the Buddha.[195] Whereas the first and second kinds of doctrine characterize the first half of the Lotus Sutra (teachings of the historical Shakyamuni), the third characterizes the latter half of the sutra (teachings of the Everlasting Original Shakyamuni). But Nichiren could see only the point stressing that Superior Practice and the other bodhisattvas who emerged from the earth were authentic disciples of the Buddha, and from that perspective he picked up and accepted the third doctrine, calling it the third teaching.[196]

Nichiren's advice in *Establishment of the Legitimate Teachings for the Protection of the Country*[197] went unheeded. Instead, suppression and exile awaited him. Gradually he grew confrontational toward the actual world and began to systematize an historicist and relativist interpretation of the sutra. We mentioned this earlier as the "five categories of teaching" (or of meaning or understanding), which are the norms of interpretation—the teaching, the hearers, the age, the country, and the sequence of propagation. These "five categories" are found in *The Teaching, Capacity, Time, and Country*[198] and in *Admonitions Against Slander*,[199] both of which were written during Nichiren's exile in Izu at the age of forty-one. Then he attempted to renew the essential teaching (*daimoku*) of the Lotus Sutra as the source of energy for reforming the world. Searching for reasons for his repeated persecutions, he gradually turned his attention to parts of the Lotus Sutra that he had earlier neglected.

He began to pay attention to the parts emphasizing bodhisattva practice that involve endurance of suffering and martyrdom. The sections that he concentrated on and frequently cited would be the second group of chapters from the perspective of the historical formation of the sutra, and the third group in terms of traditional divisions of the sutra. Nichiren frequently cited teachings from this part of the sutra in his writings from around the time of his exile on Sado Island at the age of fifty. What's more, he seems to have attempted to identify himself with Superior Practice and the other bodhisattvas who emerged from the earth, in the sense that he emphasized those who practice the Lotus Sutra. In *The Opening of the Eyes*,[200] written during his exile on Sado Island, Nichiren uses the phrase "those who practice the Lotus Sutra" twenty-six times. In *The True Object of Worship*,[201] written the following year, he selected and integrated the third division and the teaching of the Everlasting Original Buddha from the traditional division, and on the basis of the group eight chapters from 15 through 22 that overlap the two divisions, he attempted to develop his own unique doctrine. It was from this that Nichiren's unique view of the Lotus Sutra was born.

In any case, looking at the Lotus Sutra from a point of view that combines the traditional perspective with that of its historical formation, we can conclude that the sutra is comprised of three factors: (1) the true (Dharma), (2) the personal (Buddha), and (3) the human (bodhisattva). That is, the unifying truth of the cosmos corresponds to the theme of the first division (the teaching of the historical Shakyamuni), the eternal personal life to that of the second division (the teaching of the Everlasting Original Shakyamuni), and human action in this world to the theme of the third division. These three factors succinctly express the title of the Lotus Sutra—Wonderful Dharma Flower Sutra (*Saddharmapundarika Sutra*). "Wonderful Dharma" (*saddharma*) means that which defines the truth. "Sutra" means the teaching of the Buddha, thus that which is related to the Buddha. And the middle term, "Flower" (*pundarika*), signifies the bodhisattvas. The unifying truth of the cosmos is the eternally living truth of life and persons, and this is a practical truth that we ought to concretely embody in the world. This is concisely expressed in the phrase that makes up the title "Wonderful Dharma Flower Sutra," the Lotus Sutra. Therefore, Nichiren emphasized embracing the title and reciting it.

Thus, the Lotus Sutra has three characteristic ideas. Lotus Sutra and Tian-tai theory developed in distinct ways according to which of these characteristics they emphasized.

4

The Development of Lotus Sutra Thought

The Genealogy of Lotus Sutra Thought

W E HAVE ALREADY taken a quick look at how the Lotus Sutra was regarded in India. To put it simply, since Indians generally have a love for the universal, they had a high regard for the Lotus Sutra due to its emphasis on unifying truth, universality, and equality. So they paid attention to such teachings. How did this change in China? To clarify this we have to go back to the period in which many Buddhist sutras and commentaries were being translated.

Around the beginning of the fifth century, Kumarajiva, who was born near the western boundary of China, became a centrally important figure in Chinese Buddhism. His translation and introduction of many Buddhist sutras and commentaries marked a great turning point. It would be no exaggeration to say that he contributed to a revolution in thought in the Chinese Buddhist world. There were two main points involved in this change.

The first has to do with the correction of a misunderstanding of the fundamental Buddhist idea of truth—emptiness or *shunyata*—that had existed up to that time. When Buddhist sutras and commentaries were still not well known in China, the idea of emptiness was understood through the medium of ideas that already existed in China, especially the idea of nothing[202] drawn from the works of Lao-tzu and Chuang-tzu. For example, in chapter forty of the *Lao-tzu* we find: "All things emerged from being, and being emerged from nothing." Early Chinese Buddhists used the "nothing" found here to interpret the Buddhist idea of emptiness. This way of understanding Buddhism according to prior Chinese thought was later criticized for being too dependent on native terminology and struc-tures of thought.

Even before Kumarajiva's time Sinicized Buddhism had come under criticism. But he translated and introduced many sutras and commentar-ies to China, especially those that centered on explanations of emptiness, thereby making more evident the prior misunderstanding. There suddenly arose movements to correct such misunderstandings and to bring Buddhist thought into conformity with what Buddhism actually was. Sengzhao (384–414),[203] who was first among Kumarajiva's disciples in understanding emptiness, was the leading figure in this movement. His writings were later edited as *The Treatise of Zhao*.[204] By reading this book we can understand what Sinicized Buddhism was, how Sengzhao criticized it, and how with that act of criticism, he tried to clarify the true meaning of emptiness.

The second point is that once the various sutras and commentaries had been translated and introduced, there arose a demand that they be arranged and systemized—that is, that they be doctrinally interpreted. Historically speaking, the Buddhist sutras and commentaries were developed in India. If we trace them back we can sometimes come to understand their contex-tual relationships and historical order. But such procedures were not known in China, and those sutras that were first discovered were introduced and studied in a disorderly way. The need for doctrinal interpretation was born out of this disorder. Such interpretation involved appraising and ordering the sutras and commentaries according to the views of various Buddhist scholars.

This kind of interpretation flourished in the fifth and sixth centuries, during the period of the Northern and Southern dynasties. The typical inter-pretations of the three southern and seven northern teachers are introduced in the first part of the tenth chapter of Tiantai Zhiyi's *Profound Meaning of the Lotus Sutra*.[205] The most controversial issue with regard to these inter-pretations was the way in which they ordered sutras such as the Avatamsaka, Lotus, and Nirvana according to the Prajnaparamita Sutra, which teaches emptiness as the fundamental Buddhist truth. Here the Avatamsaka Sutra, which reveals the purity of truth, was defined as the "sudden teaching," the Lotus Sutra, which reveals the unity of truth, was defined as the "teaching that unifies all that is good," and the Nirvana Sutra, which reveals the eternity of truth, was defined as the "everlasting teaching." Roughly speaking, being valued most highly as the alpha and omega, the Avatamsaka Sutra and the Nirvana Sutra were placed first and last, and the Lotus Sutra was placed in the middle.

Tiantai Zhiyi, however, established his own unique interpretation, which made the Lotus Sutra supreme as "the teaching that unifies all that is good" and "the comprehensive unifying teaching." In this we can see his intention to use the Lotus Sutra to create a unifying Buddhist *summa* and to bring the disputes over interpretation to an end. He composed the work during the unification of the nation under the Sui dynasty (589–618). The establishment of a unified Buddhism indicated that there existed a comprehensive and unifying Buddhist view of truth, the world, and human life. Thus was born Tiantai Zhiyi's system of thought, comprehensive and great in both form and content.

Zhiyi found material for his interpretation of the Lotus Sutra in Daosheng's *Commentary on the Lotus Sutra*.[206] While Kumarajiva and his disciples were translating sutras and commentaries they often discussed them with each other and even sought to write commentaries on them. It seems that they set out to write such commentaries on the Lotus Sutra, but of the commentaries written by Kumarajiva's disciples only Daosheng's has survived. In any case, of the extant Chinese commentaries on the Lotus Sutra, his is the earliest, making it especially important.

In it Daosheng ponders the title of the Lotus Sutra—Wonderful Dharma Lotus Flower Sutra. In particular, he interprets "Wonderful Dharma" as being the truth that is without shape or sound, and beyond all thought. He understands "Lotus Flower'" as including both fruit and blossoms, symbolizing the idea that where there are causes there are effects. This leads him to comment that the pairing of "Lotus Flower" and "'Wonderful Dharma" signifies that the Lotus Sutra is the Dharma of wonderful cause and wonderful effect. As mentioned earlier, the sutra has been divided into two halves on the basis of cause and effect.

The law of cause and effect is a law that refers to actual existence. The fact that it is picked out here has to do with the spirit of respect for the concrete and the practical that is generally found in China. In his *Annotations on the Lotus Sutra*,[207] Fayun, who was born after Daosheng, follows his division of the Lotus Sutra into teachings of cause and effect, taking the distinction one step further. Yet where Daosheng limited the teaching of effect to the eight chapters comprising chapters 15–22, separating out the subsequent chapters as a kind of appendix, Fayun extends the teaching of effect to the end of the sutra, as did Zhiyi. We must say that, in terms of the historical formation of the sutra, dividing the sutra at chapter 22 is appropriate, and the fact that this division disappeared is regrettable. Nichiren restored this division, as mentioned earlier.

Daosheng also took it that the truth of the one vehicle reveals the teaching of cause, while the eternal life of the Buddha reveals the teaching of effect. Daosheng finds the ultimacy of the truth—teaching without remainder— in the teaching of effect. But Fayun, following this interpretation, devoted himself largely to the problem of eternity, as a consequence of which he shifted his attention from the Lotus Sutra to the Nirvana Sutra. According to Fayun, the eternity taught in the Lotus Sutra is nothing but a temporal extension of life through the divine power of the Buddha, and life will end if that divine power is exhausted. In this respect it is inferior to the eternity— the everlasting dharmakaya—taught in the Nirvana Sutra. Daosheng used the Lotus Sutra to move from various other sutras to the Nirvana Sutra ("meeting the former and opening the latter"),[208] thus making of the Lotus Sutra a kind of bridge.[209] Tiantai Zhiyi strongly opposed this idea.

There are a great many statements and writings by Tiantai Zhiyi. The most distinctive having to do with the Lotus Sutra are *Words and Phrases of the Lotus Sutra*,[210] written in 587 when he was fifty, *The Profound Meaning of the Lotus Sutra*,[211] written in 593, and the ten-fascicle *The Great Calming and Contemplation*,[212] written in 594. Together these books are known as "the three great works on the Lotus Sutra" or "the three great works of Tiantai." But they were actually all dictated by Zhiyi and recorded by his disciple Guanding (561–632),[213] and they include many of Guanding's revisions.

Words and Phrases of the Lotus Sutra is a commentary on the Lotus Sutra, with a kind of theory of interpretation. *The Profound Meaning of the Lotus Sutra* should be regarded as doctrine and doctrinal theory based on the teachings of the Lotus Sutra. *The Great Calming and Contemplation*, as a system of practice based largely on the Lotus Sutra, can be regarded as the Lotus Sutra's theory of practice. These three treatises of Tiantai gave the

Lotus Sutra a highly sophisticated and systematic structure of thought and philosophy.

Lotus Sutra Thought in Tiantai

First we should attend to the development of absolutism, centered on the understanding of "wonderful" in "Wonderful Dharma." Both Daosheng and Fayun had already given "absolute" as the meaning of "wonderful," but Zhiyi was even more thorough. In *The Profound Meaning of the Lotus Sutra* he says, "Calling the sutra 'wonderful' means that it is 'supreme.' Supreme is another name for wonderful."[214] That is, the wonderful Dharma is the supreme and absolute truth. However, Zhiyi also made the point that there are two kinds of absoluteness: relative and absolute, and thus relatively and absolutely wonderful. Thus, when he says, "If we explicate wonderful . . . first in a relative way and then in an absolute way . . ."[215] it indicates that he sees true absoluteness in a kind of absolutely wonderful.

For example, we can understand human beings to be finite and relative in contrast with God, who is infinite and absolute. But God cannot be truly absolute, as such a God is understood within the relativistic context of the dichotomy of absolute and relative—that is, his is a relative absoluteness. True absoluteness is seen where the contrast between humans and God is taken one step further. In terms of ordinary people and the Buddha, the truly absolute Buddha is such that one realizes the nonduality of extraordinary human and extraordinary Buddha and of ordinary human and ordinary Buddha. This is called "the absolutely wonderful."[216] It is absolute absoluteness.[217]

Tiantai Zhiyi maintains that the reason the Wonderful Dharma is wonderful is its true absoluteness—i.e., its absolute absoluteness—which is provisionally presupposed to be in contrast with the relative as a way of elevating wonder to a higher position. But the proper meaning of wonderful is to be found in the inconceivable transcendence of dualistic thought and judgments that distinguish between absolute and relative. "The wonderful is derived from the inconceivable. That it is so named is not due to the finite and relative."[218] Zhiyi defines it as the "nonabsolute and nonrelative" or as the "extinguishing of both relative and absolute," because it goes beyond both absolute and relative. Thus, we can say that Tiantai Zhiyi's view of absoluteness has its origin in emptiness, a fundamental Buddhist view of truth, from which he developed his view of absoluteness. In fact, he sometimes refers to the idea of emptiness and works out logical developments based on it.

The most distinctive of these is the theory of the "threefold truth" of emptiness, conventional existence, and the middle way. The theory of "threefold contemplation" is related to these three: "Entering emptiness from conventional existence; entering conventional existence from emptiness. This is the supreme meaning of the middle way."[219] He concludes the three with the integration of calming and contemplation—that is, the idea of the three contemplations in a single instant, in which emptiness, conventional existence, and the middle way are the same, identical, and simultaneous. This theory of the threefold contemplation is derived from verse 18 of the twenty-fourth chapter of Nagarjuna's *Mulamadhyamakakarika*:

> Dependent origination we declare to be emptiness. It [emptiness] is a dependent concept; just that is the middle path.[220]

This theory of the threefold contemplation is an application of what had been taught in the Sutra of the Main Business of the Bodhisattva's Jeweled Necklace,[221] a Chinese sutra believed to be from the fifth or sixth century.

Emptiness involves the negation of fixed contrapositions, such as human versus divine, ordinary people versus Buddha, evil versus good, or A versus B generally. Wherever one transcends such dichotomizing, one finds the ultimate reality of existence and of the truth—the Dharma—that supports existence. Tiantai Zhiyi's view of absoluteness began from this idea. The truly absolute God, Buddha, or Good is found where such dichotomies as those involving human beings, ordinary people, or evil are broken through or transcended. This he calls "the absolutely wonderful."

Furthermore, he developed the following kind of logic from this view of absoluteness: the relative is completely negated as relative by the relatively wonderful, and the absolutely wonderful is posited in opposition to it. This is called "breaking the relative and revealing the wonderful." Then, the relative is raised up and integrated into the absolute (the wonderful) by the absolutely wonderful. This is defined as "opening the relative and reveal-ing the wonderful." More simply put, philosophers ordinarily completely negate the human and posit an absolute God; yet we cannot say that such a posited God is truly absolute, as one can see the truly absolute God in the nonduality which goes a single step beyond the dichotomy of God and human. Put more positively, the human is embraced in the truly absolute God. This is "opening the relative and revealing the wonderful."

Looked at the other way around, we can see the divine in human beings. Returning from the absolutely wonderful of "opening the relative and revealing the wonderful" to the world of conventional reality and relative existence brings this world to life by making the absolutely wonderful alive in this world. In terms of emptiness, it is to go from the conventional duality of A and B into their nondual emptiness. Yet one does not stagnate in non-duality or emptiness but returns to the duality of conventional existence, bringing emptiness into one's life in order to have a true realization of non-duality and emptiness. This is why Zhanran, the sixth patriarch of Tiantai,[222] maintained that "nonduality is dual, and duality is nondual."[223] Small Vehi-cle Buddhists stagnated in nonduality and emptiness, forgetting to reenter the actual world and make such truth alive there. As a consequence of this they fell into deep nihilism.

We should pay careful attention to realizing that seeing the divine in the human or entering the actual world and bringing it to life is neither to affirm humanity, just as it is, as divine, nor to affirm reality, just as it is, as absolute. It is an undeniable fact that humanity is not divine, and that the actual world is finite and relative. Based on this, we have to posit the divine over against humanity, and we have to posit the absolute over against the actual. Thus, we must assert the relatively wonderful. In other words, the "abso-lutely wonderful" of "opening the relative and revealing the wonderful" does not mean to ignore such facts and affirm humanity, as it is, or to affirm the actual as absolute. In this sense, the "relatively wonderful" of "breaking the relative and revealing the wonderful" is included in "opening the relative and revealing the wonderful." Moreover, the "supreme truth of the middle way" is posited as the synthesis of "entering emptiness from conventional existence" and "entering conventional existence from emptiness." Finally, the "threefold contemplation" is taught as a conclusion—the perfect and immediate calming and contemplation of the identity of emptiness, conventional existence, and the middle way.

Thus did Tiantai Zhiyi's view of absoluteness reach its culmination. We can say that the Lotus Sutra's teaching of the unifying truth (the Wonderful Dharma of One Vehicle) gained theoretical coherence here. We can conclude that actuality is a plural, finite, and relative world. This is actuality as factual. Zhiyi insists on always acknowledging its factuality as a fact, seeing the unifying truth in it, and thereby gaining a glimpse of an absolute state. If we put this in the context of the eternal life of the Buddha revealed in chapter 16 of the Lotus Sutra, this actual life is transient—human beings live toward death. Based on this, one can realize the Everlasting Buddha, i.e., eternal life. It is in this way that one discovers the true or original Buddha.

When it came to the theory of three Buddha-bodies, Zhiyi gave primary importance to the reward body. Commenting on chapter 16, he claims that "the main theme throughout this chapter is the revelation of the three bodies. But if we take it differently, it is really concerned with the reward body. The real intention is to discuss the merits of the reward body."[224] The reward body is a figure of merit attained, in which eternal life is active in the actual world. To truly understand the reward body is to feel the throbbing life of the eternal Buddha in the midst of concrete, actual reality woven from joy and sadness, suffering and pleasure, good and evil.

With such a view of truth or theory of absoluteness—in other words, with such a view of life or theory of eternity—Tiantai Buddhists developed their own unique cosmic and world view. This is the theory of "three thousand worlds in one experience."

> A single subject holds ten dharma realms, and a single dharma realm holds ten more dharma realms, making a hundred dharma realms. There are thirty kinds of world in every realm, so a hundred dharma realms have three thousand kinds of world. These three thousand kinds of world are in a single moment of experience. If there are no experiences, there are no worlds. But if there is even a very tiny experience, it includes three thousand worlds.[225]

This expresses the idea that the unifying truth mutually penetrates the micro-world—the minimum, the single moment—and the macro-world—the maximum, the three thousand—making them into one harmonious whole. Zhiyi emphasizes the idea that a whole universe of three thousand worlds is enveloped within a micro-world of a single experience, and the micro-world of a single experience penetrates the whole universe of three thousand worlds.

First, everything in the universe is divided into ten classes or worlds, from the state of hell to the state of being a buddha. Zhiyi holds that these ten worlds do not exist independently but are interrelated, and he maintains that each of these ten worlds contains ten worlds. In this way, he posits one hundred worlds.

Furthermore, Kumarajiva's version of chapter 2 of the Lotus Sutra teaches that all things are conditioned by ten categories or factors. One hundred worlds multiplied by these ten factors makes one thousand. Further, if we look at a single thing, we can see that it is constituted by its autonomy (individual existence), the five mental and physical components which constitute it, and by its environment. The one thousand multiplied by these three spheres makes three thousand. In brief, "three thousand" is a skillful way to express the weaving together of the entire cosmos.

In contrast, a single occasion of experience can point to the smallest, infinitesimal world. It can express either an entity or a subject, something both temporally and spatially infinitesimal, and not necessarily subjective. Zhiyi insisted on this. His use of terms such as "a single experience" or "one subject" is derived from his respect for the power of engagement with existence.

With regard to mutual penetration of three thousand worlds in one occasion of experience, the following appears just after the previous quotation:

> Also, we do not say that a single subject exists first and then all things afterward, nor do we say that all things exist and then such a subject. . . . Both before and after are impossible. . . . If all things emerge from one subject, this is only the warp; if a subject includes all things in a moment, this is only the woof: either is impossible by itself. A single subject is simply all things, and all things are really one subject.[226]

Thus, one should not discuss either the three thousand things or the moment of experience from the point of view of such things as essence and appearance, real and nonreal, whole and part, or in terms of such things as temporally or spatially before and after, primary and secondary, superior and subordinate, or same and different.

The powers of all things in the universe cohere together and are united. The power of one thing, moreover, spreads out and becomes fully present within all things. If we seek the boundary of the largest universe, we will know that it is infinitely expanding. Yet at the same time, if we magnify the smallest particle with a microscope, we will know that it is the infinite, entire universe. Thus the microcosm is the macrocosm, as it is, and vice versa. "A subject is all things, and all things are subjects." The reality of this kind of world and existence is beyond our limited ability to comprehend such things as being and nonbeing or large and small. In this sense, this is a mysterious world. "Profoundly wonderful and profoundly deep, it is beyond understanding. It is beyond words. That is why it constitutes a mysterious state."[227]

As the ultimate purpose of Tiantai Zhiyi's *The Great Calming and Contemplation* is mastery of the cosmic reality of three thousand worlds in one occassion of experience, in it he develops various theories of practice and gives instructions about the various kinds of human conduct that go with these theories.

The term "calming contemplation" (*zhiguan*) is based on a compound of the Sanskrit *shamatha* (meditative calm) and *vipashyana* (contemplation). It indicates being rooted in the cosmic reality of eternity and infinity, not being upset by the changes and ups and downs of life, broadly observing the world from the perspective of such eternity and infinity, and having unattached wisdom. It is understood to be both meditation and wisdom, as the two terms together express such things as tranquility and illumination or clarity and serenity. Appropriate judgments and actions will follow from such a state.

The term *mohe* is a phonetic translation of *maha*, meaning "great." The worldview and lifeview of the *The Great Calming and Contemplation* is on an extremely large scale. It teaches a theory of practice for all kinds of situations, so it is appropriate that it is modified by the term "great." We encounter many kinds of situations and obstacles in the journey through life. *The*

Great Calming and Contemplation anticipates such situations, teaches ways of dealing with them one by one, and devises means of helping. It deals with problems of love and passion and of sin and evil, indicates what is appropriate for food and clothing, and teaches what to do about disease. We might say that it is a book of counseling that deals with all the kinds of distress and suffering experienced in life.

Moreover, whereas in Christianity arguments concerning the problem of evil focus on the relation of God and evil, in Tiantai it is the relation of Buddha and evil that is discussed. There arose a theory that there is evil in the Buddha, which proved controversial in later years. The idea that there is evil in the Buddha developed from the idea of the mutual inclusion of the ten worlds. In the idea of ten worlds, the world of the Buddha, as the world of supreme good, is located at the highest level, and the world of supreme evil, hell, is located at the lowest level. Human beings are in a middle position, caught between good and evil. Humans are intermediate beings, as emphasized in Western philosophy. But Tiantai insists that each of the ten worlds includes all of the others. Thus the world of the Buddha includes the supreme evil of hell. From this came the idea that there is evil in the Buddha, called "the theory of inherent evil."

We can see the theoretical development of this idea in Tiantai's *The Profound Meaning of the Guanyin Chapter*,[228] according to which the Buddha does not intentionally do evil (cultivated evil) but includes evil in his nature (inherent evil). There is, accordingly, the possibility of redeeming evil. Those who do not know evil are not qualified to redeem it. If we turn this theory of inherent evil around, it becomes possible to say that there is good, inherent good, in hell. From the idea of the mutual inclusion of the ten worlds, it follows that hell includes the supreme good of the Buddha's world. Thus Tiantai taught the idea that there is good naturally even in hell. In this way, Tiantai recognized that hell would someday be awakened to the good, thus being redeemed and brought up into the Buddha's world.

Put succinctly, evil and good are not permanently fixed in extreme contrast with each other. In this sense, the theory is authentically nondual. Stated positively, good and evil have things in common. *The Profound Meaning of the Lotus Sutra* says, "The nature and form of evil is really the nature and character of good. There is good because there is evil and there is no good apart from evil. . . . Evil is the origin of good. If there is no evil there can be no good.[229] . . . Evil goes together with good. But this is neither evil nor good. . . . Good goes together with evil. But this is neither good nor evil."[230]

According to the ideas of nongood and nonevil and the nonduality of good and evil, the redemption of evil is possible. Based on this, moreover, the existence of evil comes to be positively affirmed as a source of good. The existence of evil enhances the quest for the good and elevates the good itself. In this sense, without evil there is no good. This prevents human beings who are caught between good and evil from having split personalities or falling into despair.

Tiantai's theory that the Buddha includes evil in his nature or that the existence of evil is a source of good may give rise to an optimistic impression in which evil is treated lightly. There may be a danger of falling into decadence by affirming permission to do evil as one likes. In fact, later there were some who were severely criticized for understanding it in this way and putting this idea into practice. But the original intention was to try to find a possibility for salvation by looking directly at the reality of evil and hell, and grieving over it. This is neither to monistically affirm evil by seeing good and evil as having the same roots nor to deny the existence of evil.

To conclude, it is not the case that in this world there is only good and no evil. Rather, we can see the vitality of eternal life in the midst of the battle for good over evil. Through this theory of good and evil we can understand Tiantai's general view of the world and human life. We can feel the vitality of life and find its meaning in a life woven of the warp and woof of happiness and sorrow, joy and suffering, good and evil. This is why Tiantai developed views of the absolute and of eternity.

Lotus Sutra Thought in Nichiren

In Tiantai, the lamp of the Dharma was transmitted through Guanding (561–632), Zhiwei, Huiwei, and Xuanlang (673–754).[231] The later years of Guanding's life were during the time of transition from the Sui dynasty to the Tang. The home base of the Tiantai school was Mt. Tiantai, some distance south of both Chang'an (now Xi'an), the capital of that time, and from the second capital, Luoyang. Being so far from the center of power, the Tiantai school began to show signs of decline. Yet Zhanran (711–82),[232] the sixth patriarch after Zhiyi, was able to revive it.

While Zhanran was reviving the Tiantai school, Chengguan (738–839),[233] the fourth patriarch of the Huayan school, was active as well, and the two debated each other from their respective positions. The Tiantai school established its comprehensive view of the cosmos and world under its idea of unifying truth. The Huayan, on the other hand, established its ideal view of the cosmos and world under its own idea of unifying truth. These two schools, Tiantai and Huayan, present two distinctive ways of thinking about and looking at the truth and the world. Neither could be ignored.

Zhanran and Chengguan each absorbed the good points of the other while debating each other. Accordingly, after Zhanran, the Tiantai school was tinged with Huayan ways of thinking and came dangerously close to straying from fundamental Tiantai positions. During the latter half of the tenth century, during the Liao and Song dynasties, Zhili (960–1028)[234] started a movement to return to legitimate Tiantai doctrines. Zhili regarded his own position as "the mountain faction"[235] and criticized "Huayan-plated" Tiantai scholars, calling them "the off-mountain faction."[236] We can see the dispute between these two Tiantai factions as a debate between Tiantai and Huayan within the Tiantai school.

This dispute could not be resolved in China and was carried to Japan, where it was brought to an end. The reason for this is that the Lotus Sutra and the Flower Garland Sutra[237] and their ideas, in addition to all the other sutras, treatises, and ideas, came to Japan together as a group. Also, Saicho (767–822),[238] the founder of the Japanese Tiantai (Jap: Tendai) school, had first learned Huayan (Jap: Kegon) ideas and, building on them, changed the focus of his study to Tiantai's Lotus Sutra. So both Huayan and Tiantai elements were included in Japanese Tendai from the beginning. Incidentally, Daosui and Xingman[239]—disciples of Zhanran—taught Saicho when he visited China.

Saicho skillfully merged the Lotus Sutra's comprehensive and unifying view of truth with the Flower Garland Sutra's fundamental and purifying view of the truth. In his thought, the Lotus Sutra's worldview, which encompasses the actual world, is united with the worldview of the Flower Garland Sutra, which shines with the ideal. This is a unity of the ideal and the actual. In further developments along this line, thinkers after Saicho combined typical Mahayana Buddhist ideas from the Lotus Sutra, the Flower Garland Sutra, the esoteric sutras, Zen, and so forth, eventually achieving the ultimate in philosophical theory—the Tendai doctrine of original enlightenment.[240]

The Tendai doctrine of original, innate or intrinsic, enlightenment is the culmination of Buddhism, subsuming all Buddhist teachings on the basis of Tendai Lotus Sutra doctrine. In general, it makes it clear that breaking through the bounds of right and wrong, good and evil, beauty and ugliness— human relative and dualistic thought and judgment—so thoroughly breaks through that barrier that it discloses a very different absolute and monistic world. There, the boundary between heaven and earth vanishes, the distinction between above and below disappears, and only infinite cosmic space and eternal absolute time remain. From this standpoint, there is a radical affirmation that the actual world is like a dynamic pulsation of ideal light in which a moment is like an eternity. Life and death and everything else come to be affirmed as the activity of eternal life. Tendai doctrine includes such teachings as "The eternal sun and moon, today's sun and moon, and the future sun and moon are all one sun and moon," "The wonderful coming of noncoming, the true birth of nonbirth, the perfect going of nongoing, and the great death of nondeath," and "All things in the universe have the life span of the original Buddha."

The Tendai doctrine of original enlightenment was very influential, not only within Buddhism, but in Japanese thought and in the worlds of Japanese literature and art in general. Whether we agree with it or not, we cannot ignore the fact that it reigned in the background of the middle ages of Japan. The founders of the new Kamakura Buddhism, such as Honen, Shinran, Dogen, and Nichiren, were all students at Mt. Hiei at least once and learned the Tendai doctrine of original enlightenment.

As the Heian period came to a close, there was great social upheaval and strong symptoms of the evil and pollution of the end days. By the seventh year of Eisho (1052), even some ordinary people were announcing the coming of the final, degenerate period of the Dharma.[241] The age and the society proved to be finite and relative, and people were forced to realize that human beings have an evil nature and are death-bound. Faced with this kind of reality, people could not remain steeped in the world of absolutistic monism. This is why Honen (1133–1212),[242] who kept his eyes on the real world and sought its salvation, adopted the Pure Land theory of relativistic dualism and relied upon it rather than upon the absolutistic monism of the Tendai doctrine of original enlightenment. For him there was a polarization between Buddha and ordinary human beings and between the pure land and the saha world. He encouraged people to reject life in the saha world, in favor of being reborn in the pure land of the next life.

Shinran (1173–1262), Dogen (1200–1253), and Nichiren (1222–1282)[243] also came into reality out of Mt. Hiei's hall of truth. Yet their attitudes toward the actual world were quite different from Honen's. While Honen was mostly devoted to giving up on this life and longed for the pure land of the next life, Shinran, Dogen, and Nichiren struggled positively within the actual world. Their activities and writings came right after the Jokyu turbulence of 1221[244] and were related to it.

The Jokyu turbulence was the last attempt by the former dynasty to regain political power, which ended in total failure. This was the decisive event that transferred political power from the former dynasty to the newly emerging samurai warrior class. It was a kind of preparation for a period wherein the samurai would build a new order. Shinran, Dogen, and Nichiren were active in the midst of this trend. This was especially true of Nichiren, who had his home base in Kamakura, the center for the newly emerging samurai regime, and felt the new winds directly.

The birth of a new era, however, always involves trouble. The hull of the old system cannot be removed all at once, and the new powers themselves constantly experience crises from internal division. The Hojo[245] regime was exactly like this. Following a series of extraordinary natural disasters and cataclysms, it was faced with social instability. In addition, there twice occurred unprecedented attacks from outside of Japan: the Mongol raids of 1274 and 1281.

Yet these domestic and external troubles were different from the symptoms of a period of decline. They were the kind of troubles that occur as trials during times of constructive development. They were not the kind of troubles that cause one to despair or to give up on the world but the kind that produce the will to courageously confront and reform the world.

Under these circumstances, Nichiren did not understand Buddhism to be limited to saving individual souls, but rather understood it to extend to the salvation of society as a whole. Thus his hope to reform this world colored his faith in and devotion to the Lotus Sutra.

It is not hard to find reasons for this. Observing the trends and the troubles of the new age in Kamakura, Nichiren wrote his *Establishment of True Dharma for the Protection of the Country*[246] and presented it to the government. In this treatise he proclaims the unification of Buddhism based on the Lotus Sutra and gives full force to social salvation by calling for Buddhism to be united, emphasizing that the nation could only be made secure if governed by politics based on the idea of a unified Buddhism.

He focused his criticism in this work on Honen's Pure Land chanting of Amida Buddha's name. Honen's concentration on retaining the *nembutsu* as his focus of devotion, and rejecting everything else, was contrary to the unification of Buddhism that Nichiren sought. Nichiren also objected to the Pure Land *nembutsu* as an escape from the actual world. But Nichiren invited oppression upon himself by making such criticisms of Pure Land Buddhism. In 1261, at the age of forty, he was exiled to Izu Island for about two years, and in 1271 he was exiled for about three years to Sado Island. During this time he was subjected to frequent persecution, beginning his career filled with suffering.

Such cumulative suffering influenced his disciples and followers. Some could not bear it and defected. Nichiren himself agonized over such persecution and once again turned to the Lotus Sutra to seek its reasons, as a result of which he paid particular attention to the previously discussed chapters 10–22, which teach bodhisattva practice. These chapters emphasize the practice of devoting one's life completely to the sutra, even unto death. Persecution is evidence that the apostles have been sent by the Buddha to embody truth in this evil world. The sutra encourages the acceptance of suffering by understanding oneself in such a way. Experiencing this part of the sutra, Nichiren resolved his own doubts over persecution and overcame them with an apostle's martyr-consciousness, and he then redoubled his efforts to reform the world and build a good society. Devotees of the Lotus Sutra in subsequent generations inherited from Nichiren a consciousness of being a kind of chosen people—apostles reforming society—due to persecution.

In his later years, Nichiren secluded himself on Mt. Minobu and led a quiet life. He realized that it would be impossible to reform society in his own lifetime, placed his trust in the future, placed himself within a vast, infinite cosmic reality, and found peace in a state of mind that transcended this world. Yet his disciples and followers in various places carried on his mission and gave unstintingly of their lives. There have been some in premodern and modern times who, remembering Nichiren's entrustment of the future to them, developed strong activist movements, thinking it was time to reform the world and build the country.

III

The Lotus Sutra among Followers of Nichiren

5

Town Associations and Lotus Uprisings

OTH THE LOTUS SUTRA itself and its ideas have entered into and influenced every field through the ages. But here we will only discuss some followers of Nichiren, among whom we can see a variety of interesting problems and living forms of religion.

Nichizo (1269–1342),[247] a second-generation disciple of Nichiren, went to Kyoto in the spring of 1294 to do missionary work. Beginning here, the Lotus (or Nichiren) School[248] developed and grew in the Kyoto area. Nichizo was expelled from Kyoto three times because he was so aggressive in his missionary activities. But in 1321 he founded the first Nichiren temple in Kyoto, Myokenji,[249] with the merchants, craftsmen, and ordinary townspeople that he had gradually been able to influence.

Due to support from merchants and craftsmen, the Nichiren School in Kyoto strengthened and grew. Nichiju (1314–92),[250] a monk who went to Kyoto in 1381, for example, gained the support of merchants, renovated a merchant's house, and in 1383 built Myomanji temple.[251] The Nichiren School strengthened its influence especially within self-governing cooperative associations of townspeople. In other words, the Nichiren School grew because of the town associations.

Merchants and weavers around the Sanjo, Shijo, and Shichijo, and people under the protection of the local gods of the Gion and Inari Shrines, soon became followers of Nichiren. The townspeople protected their towns and way of life through cooperative defense, military power, and combat, quite like uprisings martialed by farmers who followed the True Pure Land School.[252] These were called "Lotus Uprisings."

In those days, the Rinzai Zen School, under the protection of the

Kamakura Shogunate, was the most powerful in Kyoto. But according to records of the Nichiun faction of Nichiju, the Nichiren School became the second most popular. The records say, "Second to the Zen School, the Lotus School seems to be flourishing."[253] With the support of townspeople the Lotus School was prospering second only to the Zen School by 1400. By about 1460, most of the townspeople in Kyoto had joined the Nichiren School, until finally the Lotus faithful filled Kyoto. In connection with this, the number of temples in Kyoto belonging to the Nichiren School grew to around sixty by around 1440. Twenty-one of these were head temples with their own branch temples.

In 1532, when a Lotus Uprising went to Yamashina in southeast Kyoto to attack and burn the Hongan-ji temple, there were more than ten thousand people in the mob, including more than four hundred mounted cavalrymen. The procession packed the city's streets. This Lotus Uprising, the so-called "Tenmon Lotus Rebellion,"[254] continued to control the city of Kyoto, until it was attacked and defeated in July of 1536 by priest-soldiers from Mt. Hiei.

This is how in those days the Nichiren group developed into a town movement, while the True Pure Land Buddhist group developed into a farmers' movement. As the Kamakura period gave way to the Muromachi period, the estate system of the nobility[255] collapsed and was replaced by powerful regional lords,[256] who seized the right to rule in the provinces. At the same time, the farmers rose up and formed their own cooperative associations. Thus, the so-called village system came into being. The farmers held meetings, made rules, used their own strength to protect their way of life, and tried to manage their villages, even at times taking up arms to defend themselves.

True Pure Land Buddhism seeped into such villages. Faith in True Pure Land Buddhism was deepened by its style of missionary work. They held gatherings with the idea that followers and fellow seekers belong together. This fit well with the village system, and many True Pure Land Buddhists lived in areas where it developed. The most distinguished of these was Rennyo (1415–99),[257] the eighth abbot of Honganji.[258] In 1471, Rennyo moved into Yoshizaki in the Echizen district and, using the district as a home base, aggressively propagated the faith all around the Hokuriku area.

As gatherings of True Pure Land Buddhist believers grew, uprising movements also grew, borrowing from their organization. The so-called "Ikko Uprisings"[259] of True Pure Land Buddists were part of this. The Ikko Uprisings occurred everywhere, but on the largest scale in 1488 in Kaga, where the sheriff had to commit suicide. After that, the system of rule by consultation with the farmer-followers of True Pure Land Buddhism continued for about a whole century. The power of the Ikko Uprisings gradually spread throughout the Kinki (Kansai) area, eventually coming into conflict with the Lotus Uprisings.

The doctrines of True Pure Land Buddhism were not a direct driving force behind the Ikko Uprisings, but they did have an indirect effect. The teaching that one can be reborn after death in the pure land helped farmers to fight without fear. With the assurance of being reborn in paradise, and supported by the organization of the True Pure Land Buddhist brotherhood, farmers united and were able to create a resistance movement against the establishment.

In contrast, the people in towns became especially devoted to the Lotus Sutra, strongly tied to doctrines taught by Nichiren. The sutra's emphasis on engaged practice in this world, the aggressive attitude toward this world present among the group of Nichiren priests, and their vigorous world-affirming spirit coincided well with the emotions of merchants and craftsmen, who worked very hard in order to make a profit. Here we can see a good example of the skillful combination of profit-making cooperative groups and spiritual cooperative groups that resulted in an increase in the number of Nichiren followers.

6

The Martyrdom of the Fuju-fuse

THERE EXISTS ANOTHER event in premodern Japan—aside from the persecution of Christians—that was colored with the blood of martyrs. It concerns a group of Nichiren priests called the *Fuju-fuse* faction.[260] Disparaged under the Tokugawa shogunate as "the enemy of the world and the object of the enmity of all people," the Fuju-fuse sect was prohibited, along with the Christians, and was fiercely persecuted until the third year of the Meiji period (1871). The martyrs' blood shed by this group is more than enough to refute Christian critics who claim that there were no Buddhist martyrs.

The word *fuju* of Fuju-fuse means "not receiving services from those who do not share the same faith." The word *fuse* means "not giving services to priests who are not of the same faith." We can discern from this that all of the followers of Fuju-fuse were involved in martyrdom. Such a severe life of faith started with the founder, Nichiren. Believing that the Lotus Sutra was the supreme and absolute truth, Nichiren preached that all people should come home to it, and that those who did not should be vigorously persuaded (broken down)[261] and shown no charity.

Nichiren's fiercely confrontational way, his admonitions to the government to wake up, and his direct appeal to the government for a change in power invited a number of suppressions in his own time. Following his death, for example, in 1398 Nichinin, Nichijitsu,[262] and others from Myomanji Temple in Kyoto made admonitions directly to the Shogun Yoshimochi, which resulted in their being captured, beaten, and tortured by having water constantly poured into their mouths and boiling water poured over their heads.

Nisshin (1407–88)[263] of the Nakayama sub-sect[264] went to Kyoto at the age of twenty-one, where he frequently rebuked the government. He was finally captured in 1440 by Shogun Yoshinori and made to undergo torture by fire and water, and other tortures beyond description. His penis was pierced with bamboo skewers, hot farm implements were put under his arms, the tip of his tongue was cut off, and finally a red-hot pot was put over his head, all of which he endured, gaining the popular nickname "Pot-Crowned Nisshin."

In 1608, Nikkyo[265] of Jorakuin[266] was supposed to engage in a debate with Pure Land monks at Edo Castle, but on the night before the debate he was assaulted by a mob and badly injured. His disciples begged to have the debate postponed but were refused. Since he could not speak, it was ruled that Nikkyo's side lost the debate, and Nikkyo himself was ordered to write an apology and admission of defeat. He refused, arousing the wrath of Shogun Ieyasu. The next year he was severely punished at the Rokujo-gawara in Kyoto by having his nose and ears sliced off. One of his disciples lost his life. In the Nichiren school this was called suffering for the Dharma in the Keicho period.[267]

Some Nichiren priests prepared themselves for torture with daily ascetic training. But oppression grew more severe with the establishment of the unified regimes of Oda, Toyotomi, and Tokugawa. Eventually the great majority of those in the Nichiren School took the course of softening their stance. But the Fuju-fuse sect never compromised, eagerly sticking to the way of martyrdom until the end.

The Fuju-fuse martyrdom had its beginnings in 1595, when Hideyoshi Toyotomi, the extremely powerful general and ruler of most of Japan, wanted to hold a thousand-monk ceremony for the dedication of the great Buddha statue at Hokoji in Kyoto,[268] in which monks from various schools were invited to take part. The great majority of Nichiren school monks were inclined to accept the invitation. Only Nichio (1565–1630)[269] of Myokakuji[270] refused, claiming that, just as there was no reason to be charitable to nonbelievers, one should refuse to receive support from them. He sent a rebuke to Hideyoshi from the Lotus School,[271] recommending that the ceremony be cancelled. Afraid that this would bring a lot of trouble to the temple, he ran away during the night and became a wanderer. Nichio was from the merchant class; even as a monk something of their spirit remained in his blood.

Everywhere he went in his wanderings, Nichio continued to criticize those who had agreed to participate in the ceremony. Thus the conflict between the Fuju-fuse and Ju-fuse sect, which accepted the invitation to participate, came to a head. In 1599 Nichio was summoned before Tokugawa Ieyasu on a complaint made by the Ju-fuse sect, and he was exiled the next year to the island of Tsushima.[272] Pardoned in 1612, he returned to the capital. But the fight between the two sects continued to intensify. In 1630, by order of the Shogunate, Nichio was once again banished to Tsushima. He died in March of the same year, before the sentence could be carried out. So his remains were sent in exile to Tsushima instead, a so-called "posthumous banishment." Six other monks were exiled along with the ashes of Nichio.

But the Fuju-fuse sect only became more and more popular, driving the Shogunate to set up measures to thoroughly suppress it. They demanded that Fuju-fuse temples show receipts for their buildings and lands, and even for roads and drinking water, claiming that they belonged to the state. Unless the temples obeyed, the government would do such things as forbid them from issuing registration certificates to parishioners, or banish their monks. If Fuju-fuse parishioners could no longer receive certificates from the temples, they would be unable to demonstrate their registration as long as they held to their faith, in effect becoming illegals, excluded from society. Some of the monks went out to preach in the town, but the Shogun banned even that.

Most of the Fuju-fuse monks went underground, taking up a life of wandering. Most of the followers became Ju-fuse, officially registering at other temples but secretly continuing in their hearts to believe in the Fuju-fuse teachings. The most ardent Fuju-fuse followers became illegal, homeless, ostracized people trying to live by a pure faith consistent with their hearts. Many abandoned their homes or lost their lives.

They secretly held meetings at night, chanting sutras or listening to sermons in underground storehouses or remote rooms with lookouts on guard. Still, they never knew when they would be apprehended. When they gathered together they always wore travelling clothes to escape in, and they put their important documents in secret places, such as bamboo containers hanging from rafters, inside the walls or pillars of a house, or in clay jars buried deep in the ground. Monks concealed a proclamation in an inner pocket, intending if caught to make a last rebuke of the government before giving up their lives.

Even with such skillful underground precautions, spies managed to infiltrate the sect. Both monks and lay followers were frequently caught, the number of those captured becoming very high. In one incident in 1668, the monk Nikkan[273] of the temple Myogakuin[274] was caught hiding in the house of a follower in Yatabe (now in Okayama Prefecture). He was arrested along with five of his dedicated followers, who gave themselves up along with their families. Nikkan and the five followers, all young men in their thirties, had their heads chopped off, and the twenty-eight family members—many of them women, including wives, sisters, daughters, maids, and even one- and two year-old children—were all exiled.

The following year, Nikkan's master, Nissei,[275] was required to sign a receipt for the roads and drinking water that had been donated to the temple. Deciding that he had little hope in this world, he shut himself up in a cave in Fukuda (in present-day Tsuyama City) and devoted himself to fasting and chanting praises to the Lotus Sutra. Before long four women followers joined him. They all died together from starvation. In addition to such cases, others often lived by their faith and ended up committing suicide.

In 1691, a great roundup was made across the country, and sixty-three monks and eleven followers were exiled to islands such as Miyake-jima, O-shima, Kozu-shima, Nii-jima, and Hachijo-jima. Some died in prison and others committed suicide. The graves of these monks and articles left behind by them still remain on these islands. Some islanders were converted and several preserved in their houses statues of Shakyamuni and of Nichiren, mandalas, copies of the Lotus Sutra, and such given to them by the exiled monks.

The government became even more strict and oppressive during the critical stage at the end of the feudal Tokugawa period. One such result was the Tenpo Persecution.[276] The government made a massive roundup of Fuju-fuse members and the group was virtually wiped out. The remaining members, barely surviving, kept the faith by being very careful—doing such things as using code numbers for their gathering places and names. But they could not escape the search altogether. The storm of oppression continued until the third year of the Meiji period, 1871.

What on earth drove Fuju-fuse members, even feeble women and little children, to such devotion without regard for their bodies or lives? This, like the martyrdom of Christians, has to be one of the mysteries of history. They may have found direct support in the idea of being a kind of chosen people—the Lotus Sutra's emphasis of the apostle's sense of completely devoting one's life to one's faith, even unto death. On the other hand, their reason for such ardor may have to do with their social background. One can criticize the doctrines, contentions, and actions of the Fuji-fuse from a contemporary perspective, but even taking such criticism into account, we have to admire their pure and noble religious faith.

7
Nationalist Faith among Modern Japanese Followers of Nichiren

I N MODERN TIMES in Japan, from the beginning of the Meiji period, Lotus Sutra faith, or Nichirenism, has been roughly of three types. The first, a nationalistic type of faith, accompanied the rise of contemporary nationalism and tried to make Nichiren a pillar of Japanese nationalism. The second, a type of faith that transcends the national and is based instead on the "universal individual," is the opposite of the first—in other words, it espouses a reverence for cosmic reality through the person of Nichiren and faith in the Lotus Sutra. The third is the type of faith found among the popular groups at the center of the new religions movement.

Chigaku Tanaka (1861–1939)[277] is most representative of the first, nationalistic type of Nichiren faith. Firmly believing that enhancement of the nation should be of primary concern to any Nichiren movement, he developed his own unique Nichiren movement, bound up in the rising nationalism of the time. He founded several nationalistic organizations, the most famous and lasting of which is the Pillar of the Nation Association.[278]

One might say that Tanaka developed his thought and action based on Nichiren's *Establishment of True Dharma for the Protection of the Country*, but Nichiren's main point in that work was to establish the true Dharma (*rissho*). It may be that national security (*ankoku*) is a natural product of establishing the true Dharma, but this is not the main purpose for doing so. This is evident in the way in which Nichiren structured the book. It consists of a dialogue between a master (the sacred), who is set on true Dharma, and a visitor (the secular), who is set on securing the nation. Nichiren develops the story so as to gradually lead the visitor to the position of the master.

If someone had asked Tanaka which was most important—establishment of the true Dharma or the security of the nation—of course, he would have said the former. Yet he tended to absolutize Japan in the way in which he connected the nation to the true Dharma (the Lotus Sutra). Consequently, his Nichirenism was linked with nationalism. This was a serious problem. However, we should take into consideration that it was really his love and concern for the nation that forced him to be like this. In fact Tanaka's passionate advocacy brought him wide influence. Many, especially among the military and the far right, wanted to become his disciples. As a result of this interest on the right, some attribute attempted right-wing military coups to the influence of his Nichirenism and his interpretation of the Lotus Sutra.

Ikki Kita (1883–1937)[279] was the mastermind behind the attempted military coup of February 26, 1936, in Japan. He readily attached himself to the idea of being a chosen-apostle found in the Lotus Sutra and in Nichiren's thought, and this became the driving force behind his sense of mission with regard to the Japanese and Chinese revolutions. While most right-wing activists put the emperor above the nation, Kita put the nation above the emperor. In *National Polity and Pure Socialism*[280] he says that the emperor is "one element of the state, equal to the people, who are other elements, in being an organ of the state." He maintained that the substance of sovereignty was the nation, not the emperor. So he advocated a "patriotism that arises from loyalty to the nation" and came to the conclusion that loyalty should be given to the nation.

Kita wrote *An Unofficial History of the Chinese Revolution*,[281] which he published in 1921, expressing his convictions about and aspirations for the Chinese revolution. It is interesting that he regularly cites ideas from Nichiren and expressions from the Lotus Sutra in this book. For example, at the end of the preface he says, "The sutra says that the earth trembled and split open and bodhisattvas sprang up from below the earth," referring to the story in chapter 15 of the Lotus Sutra. He maintains that trembling and splitting open signifies "events such as the emerging of the world revolution" and that the bodhisattvas who emerged from the earth were "a crowd of saviors hidden under a layer of earth," "heroes in the swamp grass," and the "great people of the lower class fighting for righteousness."

Kita concludes the book, writing, "Without following the great way of the universe, the Lotus Sutra, China will remain in darkness forever. In the end, India has not become independent. Japan, too, will perish. The eight rolls of the Lotus Sutra reward or punish the rights or wrongs of a nation. Who can testify for Shakyamuni Buddha in the final days, using the sword of the Dharma as a walking stick?"

On the day before he was to be executed for complicity in the February 26 incident, Kita wrote some farewell words to his son on the back of a copy of the Lotus Sutra that he had kept with him to the end: "I leave only this Lotus Sutra to you, my son. When you remember me, when you miss me, when you become sad in the midst of your life journey, when you have lost your way, when you are troubled by anger, envy, or resentment, and when you are happy or pleased, pray and chant *Namu myoho renge kyo* before this Lotus Sutra."

Here we sense a feeling similar to Nichiren's when he said: "Realize sorrows as sorrows, let joys be joys, take sorrows and joys together, and chant *Namu myoho renge kyo*." Yet Nichiren and Kita differed significantly in their ideas of the nation. For Nichiren, the nation was above the emperor, and the Dharma was above the nation. The Dharma, the realm of the Buddha, is sacred and universal, something beyond this secular world. The authority of the emperor and the power of the nation can be criticized from that position, and this can become a source of power for negation and change. Kita is like Nichiren in putting the nation above the emperor, but he stopped there. As a consequence, he made the nation into an absolute.

Nichiren's idea was to regulate and reform the nation from a position that transcends it. This was a fundamental principle for him. But this principle was split when it was applied in the modern world: leaning toward transcending the nation on the one hand and toward nationalism on the other. Nichiren's principle may have parted in these two directions because Japan, in its national infancy at the time, was still newly wrestling with the modern questions of how religion should relate to the state and how the state, in turn, should relate to society.

Nichiren had predicted that in the final days of the Dharma "an unprecedented, great worldwide conflict" would occur, and he emphasized that the world would then be united by the supreme truth of the Lotus Sutra. Kanji Ishihara (1889–1949),[282] an army general, applied Nichiren's words such as these to the situation in East Asia and the world at that time. In May of 1940, he gave a lecture on "The Theory of the Final World War," and later that year wrote the *Survey of the Origins of Histories of Wars*,[283] in which he said, "Saint Nichiren revealed the great war for the unification of the world."

Ishihara hoped for cooperation and racial friendship between Japan and China in order to prepare for the final world war. With this in mind he worked for the creation of the Manchurian state. The Association for the Union of East Asia was formed in November of 1939, and branches opened all over Japan and China. It spread to such an extent that even a Student Union of East Asia was established in June of 1940, and the thirty-four major Japanese universities joined it. But as hostilities between China and Japan increased, a Sino-Japanese war loomed larger. Ishihara warned of the recklessness of a Sino-Japanese war and tried as much as he could to stop its expansion.

8

Transnational Faith among Modern Japanese Followers of Nichiren

I N CONTRAST WITH the nationalism of the first kind of Nichirenism, there were some among the followers of Nichiren and the Lotus Sutra who embraced a transnational faith in their lives. Chogyu Takayama (1871–1902)[284] argued that Buddhism was a world religion and in that sense had the same viewpoint as Christianity. Therefore it should go hand in hand with Christianity in opposing Nipponism "as the common enemy of Buddhism and Christianity."

Later, Takayama had a chance to reflect during his convalescence from tuberculosis, during which time his attention was attracted to the idea of the realm of the universal individual, who transcends nation and race and places his trust in a sacred religious realm that transcends the secular world. He subsequently happened to get ahold of Tanaka's book, *Reformation of the Sect*,[285] which turned his attention to Nichiren.

Studying Nichiren, Takayama's eyes gradually began to open to the sacred and religious, which transcends nations, and he came to understand the elite mindset that derives from the sense of there being a sacred realm that transcends the authority of nations. He adopted such a mindset himself, overcame his tuberculosis-related depression, and gained a newfound pride and joy in living. Though he had fallen into depression when crushed by disease, Takayama was deeply encouraged by Nichiren's valiant attitude as a "practitioner of the Lotus Sutra" who did not flinch at the hardships of life or at the authority of the nation.

In June of 1902 Takayama published *Saint Nichiren and the Nation of Japan*,[286] in which he claimed that those who regarded Nichiren as a nationalist were mistaken. He argued, "Nichiren accepted the nation for the sake of the truth, not vice versa," "For Nichiren the truth was greater than the nation," and "He even approved of the destruction of the nation for the sake of the truth." In this sense, Nichiren, rather than having the so-called spirit of loyalty to the emperor and love for the nation, "was highly disloyal." Takayama became angry when he saw the way in which Nichiren priests were turning Nichiren into a nationalist just as nationalism was on the rise in Japan. In the essay quoted above he wrote, "Alas! It is terribly unfortunate that priests attempt to show pride in the prosperity of their own school under the pretext of identifying it as the national religion. Saint Nichiren is praised as a nationalist by the very mouths of such evil priests. How sad!" Though Tanaka's *Reformation of the Sect* had inspired Takayama, he grew skeptical of Tanaka's views of the nation. He sent a letter to Tanaka saying something like, "I have respectfully and carefully listened to and read your opinions about Saint Nichiren's views of the nation. Yet many difficult unresolved problems remain."

Among those who were transnationalist Nichiren devotees, some were only slightly different from Takayama. They moved toward the cosmic faith taught by the Lotus Sutra and mediated by Nichiren. One such devotee was Kenji Miyazawa (1896–1933),[287] a poet, writer of children's stories, and agricultural scientist. Around his final year of high school, he happened to come across the book *The Lotus Sutra in Chinese and Japanese*[288] by Daito Shimaji[289] in his own house. He read it through once and was immediately thrilled by it. From then on he gradually grew more and more devoted to the Lotus Sutra and, without doing so explicitly, often incorporated its teachings into his stories. He was often explicit in his letters. For example, in a letter written just before his graduation from high school, he wrote, "*Namu myoho renge kyo! Namu myoho renge kyo!* I sincerely offer myself in service to the Sutra of the Lotus Flower of the Wonderful Dharma, the foundation of the greatest happiness for all. When I chant 'Praise to the Lotus Sutra' just once, the world and I are enveloped in a wondrous light."

When he was twenty-five, Miyazawa joined Tanaka's Pillar of the Nation Association, and in the following year he went to Tokyo to look into the organization and devote himself to being a follower of Nichiren. Miyazawa's admiration for Tanaka and Nichiren was abnormally passionate, as can be seen in the letters he wrote to friends in 1920, when he joined the Pillar of the Nation Association. "I joined the Practice of Faith Division of the Pillar of the Nation Association. In other words, my life now belongs to Saint Nichiren. Thus I am now under the direction of Professor Chigaku Tanaka."

Miyazawa's sister, Toshi, whom he loved more than anyone else in the world, died from tuberculosis when he was twenty-seven. In his poems from that time we begin to see signs of change in his fervent faith as a Nichiren follower. He began to move toward a cosmic faith through the Lotus Sutra. A few years later, in the preface to a book on the art of farming,[290] he wrote, "To live a strong and righteous life is to hold the whole galaxy in one's awareness and to act accordingly." In the book itself he says, "Together let us first spread out in the sky in all directions by becoming radiant specks of cosmic dust." His reverence for cosmic reality is evident in this encouragement to put oneself in an infinite cosmic context.

Miyazawa's view of the cosmos wasn't abstract or static but practical, volitional, and active. He said, "Burn all problems as you would firewood, and be sympathetic with the spirit in all things," and "Gather energy from the clouds by communicating with the winds." In conclusion he emphasized, "What we need is a clear will that embraces the galaxy—such great energy and heat." He ties "energy from the clouds," "clear will that embraces the galaxy," and "great energy and heat" together in the "great quest" for the sake of the world. "First of all, let's have the great quest for the sake of the world," he wrote, indicating that "the great quest" is that the whole world become happy. "Until the whole world becomes happy, there can be no individual happiness," he explains, and, "Our quest is for the true happiness of the world." One is reminded here of the bodhisattva practice of the Lotus Sutra. Miyazawa learned these lessons for living—bathing in the galaxy, taking energy from that, seeking the happiness of the whole world, and burning ordinary problems like firewood while living a strong and righteous life of shared suffering and joy—from the Lotus Sutra. He often said, "Live a strong and righteous life. Move onward without avoiding suffering."

Miyazawa's source for this was the Sutra of the Lotus Flower of the Wonderful Dharma. For him, that was where the spring of true happiness emerges, and where one finds the source of energy for realizing happiness. In a letter he wrote, "We should have great courage and seek true happiness for all living beings. This is the Lotus Sutra." Occasionally he chanted *Namu myoho renge kyo* and imagined that his spirit was flying in the boundless sky, where he was filled with the joy of a transcendent life, and from which he returned to earth having acquired strength and courage to endure a life of suffering.

Miyazawa took up an extremely stoic life, wearing plain clothes and eating simple food. At the age of thirty-three, in addition to being overworked, he came down with the tuberculosis that would soon kill him. In February of the following year, looking his own death in the face, he wrote poems beginning with the following words:

> I will die soon
> today or tomorrow.
> Again, anew, I wonder, "What am I?"

And he ended this way:

> The original Dharma of all the buddhas is nothing but
> the Lotus Flower of the Wonderful Dharma Sutra.
> Praise to the Lotus Flower of the Wonderful Dharma Sutra.
> Life, too, is the life of the Wonderful Dharma.
> Death, too, is the death of the Wonderful Dharma.
> In life and in death I uphold the Wonderful Dharma.[291]

The view of life and death in these closing words is in much the same vein as that of Tendai original enlightenment thought introduced earlier. Yet Tendai original enlightenment thought was so taken up with absolute states that it forgot the reality of actual death, and in turn tended to fall into idealistic and monistic affirmation of actual reality. Compared with it, there was fear and trembling in Miyazawa's existential gaze at death. In a piece called "Night," from April 28[292] of the same year as the poems above, he wrote:

So far, for two hours
the blood from my throat hasn't stopped.
Outside, people walk no longer.
Trees quietly breathe and bud on this spring night.
This very place is spring's place of practice.

The bodhisattva has discarded a billion of his bodies.
The many buddhas here experience life and nirvana. And so
tonight, now, here, seen by no one,
I can die alone.

I've held this thought many times,
telling it to myself.
But once again lukewarm
new blood wells up. And
once again pale-white, I become frightened.

An appointment book that he apparently wrote in while on his deathbed was found after he died. Words and phrases from the Lotus Sutra were written all over it, and in it we can see his readiness for death. On the inside of the back cover, written in Chinese, are the words from chapter 21 of the Lotus Sutra: "You should understand that all such places are places of the Way. . . . They are where the buddhas reach complete nirvana."[293] This was one of Nichiren's favorite passages, one that he read often. It is also one that Dogen chanted when he was seriously ill.

From this note we can see that Miyazawa's previously overeager faith had receded into the shadows. In its place we see an introspective and humble attitude. This is recorded, for example, in the following poem:

I do not want pleasure.
I do not want fame.
Now I just
want to offer
this base, useless body
to the Lotus Sutra;

to light up a speck of dust
and, if forgiven,
become a servant to my father and mother,
to return their billions of favors.
Sick and faced with death,
I have no other wish.

This famous poem dated November 3, is written in his appointment book:

Neither yielding to rain;
Nor yielding to wind.

He also said that he wanted to be

What everyone calls a good-for-nothing,
No one praises
And no one worries about—
This is the kind of man
I want to be.[294]

On the day before his death on September 20, 1933, he wrote a poem that said:

I will be glad if my life
Rotting away from disease
Results in some fruit.

Once again so sick that he couldn't get up, he was crushed with grief, fell into depression, and was gripped by a sense of failure. But his faith in the Lotus Sutra was strengthened, and he lived a solid life to the end despite being very sick, often helping poor peasants with fertilizer problems, while enveloped by the infinite cosmos and embraced by eternal life.

On September 21, 1933, ready to meet death, he chanted the *daimoku* and left some final words for his father saying that he wanted to send a thousand copies of the Japanese translation of the Lotus Sutra to his acquaintances.

Inside the back cover he wanted him to write words to the following effect: "My whole life's work has been to deliver this sutra to you. I hope you will enter the supreme Way by coming in contact with the will of the Buddha."

9

People-Centered Faith—
Socialist Followers of Nichiren

L AST TO BE discussed is a group among the new religious movements of Japan that have a people-centered faith. Twentieth century
new religious movements in Japan can be divided broadly into two
kinds: Shinto and Buddhist. Almost all the Buddhist groups are related to
Nichiren or Lotus faith. These new religious organizations were flourishing
until recent years, with anywhere from a few hundred thousand to several
million members.

What are the reasons for this flourishing? The answer is related for the
most part to three common characteristics of the new religious movements,
which put simply are thanksgiving (*okage*), being cursed (*tatari*), and correction (*naoshi*). Thanksgiving involves receiving benefits in this world.
Being cursed has to do with the worship of ancestor spirits, as it is understood that present unhappiness is caused by curses from restless ancestor
spirits. And correction, which includes social reform, making fresh starts,
and restoration of everyday life, involves improvement and reform of society. Of these three common characteristics, it is thought that thanksgiving
and being cursed are rooted in ancient Japanese ways of thinking. We know
from ancient myths that the Japanese were very strongly oriented to this
world and had a strong animistic interest in ancestor worship. This interest
underlies all of Japanese history. On the other hand, correction, especially
social reform, is related to the social background in which the new religious
movements arose.

We find harbingers of the new religious movements, of both the Shinto
and Buddhist types, at the end of the Tokugawa period. The earliest among

the Shinto groups was the Fuji-ko,[295] organized from the mountain-worshipping Fuji faith. The Assembly Established by the Buddha[296] was a Nichiren group founded by Seifu Nagamatsu (1817–90).[297] At thirty-two, Nagamatsu, born as the son of townspeople in Kyoto, became the Buddhist priest Nissen[298] in the Eight-chapter Faction of the Lotus Sect[299] (now the Main Gate School of the Lotus Sect).[300] Later, he decided that it was necessary to return to lay life, where he organized a lay-oriented group called the "Assembly Established by the Buddha."

We find the three characteristics mentioned earlier in the new religious movements that appeared at the end of the Tokugawa period. Correction, especially social reform, was related to and continued in the popular movements that peaked at the end of the period, known by such names as "pilgrimage of thanksgiving"[301] and "Why not?"[302] As the Tokugawa period drew to a close, group pilgrimages to the Ise Shrine became popular, pilgrimages of thanksgiving largely being the reason for this. These pilgrimages were also called "pilgrimages of slipping away,"[303] indicating that they sometimes involved sneaking away from family or employer without permission to go on a pilgrimage to the Ise Shrine. Such pilgrimages were called "pilgrimages of thanksgiving" because pilgrims were given food and lodging by people along the way.

Pilgrimage to Ise, where the Ise Grand Shrine is located, initially became popular during the Muromachi period (1392–1573) when this pilgrimage was known for its atmosphere of pleasure. From the seventeenth century on, it took the form of group pilgrimage, and in the eighteenth century it developed into a large-scale movement involving the whole country. Rumors that Ise Shrine talismans had fallen from heaven spread widely, and groups from several hundred thousand to several million made pilgrimages to the Ise Shrine. Records show that the number of people making pilgrimages of thanksgiving in 1830 reached a total of 4,862,088.

Pilgrimages of thanksgiving allowed people to express their frustrations and provided some temporary release. They were a kind of passive resistance to the feudal regime. In fact, there were cases in which such pilgrimages transformed into definite resistance movements in the form of riots and uprisings. One case in which such pilgrimages turned into a kind of social reform movement was the popular wild dance of the "Why not?" movement that occurred in the fall and winter of 1867. The movement was initiated in late August by a rumor in the Nagoya area that Ise Shrine talismans had fallen from heaven. Men and women, young and old, went crazy with joy and danced wildly. By October, this exuberance had spread over much of Japan, from the Kyoto-Osaka area, through the areas along the Tokaido highway from Kyoto to Edo (Tokyo), to such places as Edo itself, Kofu, Matsumoto, Tokushima, and Fukushima. This was just at the time when the Tokugawa government came to an end, returning control of the country to the emperor. The faction that overthrew the Tokugawa shogunate encouraged and took advantage of the "Why not?" movement among the people.

The people, expecting social reform and stirred up by the words "Why not? Why not?," danced around in the streets day and night with fanfare, disguised in strange costumes of the opposite sex. In the process, groups would push their way into the homes of long-disliked landlords or rich merchants, taking wine and money, and chanting, "Why not have this?" When they got sleepy, they slept, not caring whether or not they were in a stranger's house. And when they woke up, they resumed dancing and chanting, "Why not? Why not?"

Pilgrimages of thanksgiving, especially the "Why not?" movement, were an outlet for the dissatisfactions of suppressed people, which they turned to in a kind of religious ecstasy. Some feared that the excitement and trance of such religious ecstasy would make people lose their minds and drive them to immoral acts. Further, since these movements were not organized, lacked leaders, and were driven by mass psychology, it would have been difficult for them to exercise any unified power to accomplish anything as a group.

A mass movement that was clearly organized and well-directed was the so-called "new religions movement." Consequently, some of the new religions have been able to engage in various kinds of social reform. In some of the new religions, the social reform element was weaker than those of thanksgiving involving this-worldly benefits or of being cursed by ancestor spirits. But on the other hand, some of the new religious groups do advocate social reform.

The new religious movements developed from the alienated class or lowest social stratum of society—in other words, so-called oppressed peoples grew frustrated and exploded. They emphasized the idea that if a new religious group grew, its teachings spread, and if the world was reformed, a happier world would emerge with the people at its center. A lot of people were brought into new religious movements in this way.

In a typical society, people at the lowest level can gain status by participating in religious organizations and experiencing the comforts and joys of the group. This is a kind of acquisition of special social identity through religious faith. Groups that managed to instill such identity gained many followers. Among the new Buddhist religious organizations, Nichiren and Lotus Sutra groups, such as Soka Gakkai,[304] Rissho Kosei-kai,[305] and Reiyu-kai,[306] were dominant. This was a consequence of the fact that they found in Nichiren and in the Lotus Sutra a social identity and an idea of social reform. Of course, we cannot ignore the influence of a positive attitude toward this world and the idea of gaining benefits in this world, which were the most prominent characteristic of such groups.

Chogyu Takayama, discussed earlier, also gained a special social identity through Nichiren, but in his case we might see social identity as a kind of sacred identity. In new religious movements such a sense of identity created a sacred group through a process of socialization. Generally speaking, such groups provide a sense of fellowship, something that is a great support for people.

Further, there was a group of socialistic followers of Nichiren within the popular social reform movements, which became politicized—the so-called "left wing" Nichiren movement. Movements such as that initiated by Giro Senoo[307] were of this kind. Senoo was born into a sake-producing family in Hiroshima in 1890. He entered the Ichiiko High School, but he got tuberculosis and dropped out of school. He fought against the disease for over ten years. While recuperating he became a follower of Nichiren and later joined Nissho Honda's (1867–1931)[308] Toitsukaku group.[309]

Honda was a priest in the Kempon Hokke-shu[310] who inspired turning the image of Nichiren toward nationalism, and like Chigaku Tanaka was very influential. A number of prominent men of the time praised Honda's 1916 book, *Lectures on the Lotus Sutra*.[311] Honda was expelled from the sect at one time because of his effort to reform it. But he returned to the fold and was head abbot for a long time, contributing to the movement for the unification of Nichiren sects. In addition to founding the Toitsukaku in

1912, he founded various organizations, such as the Tenseikai in 1909,[312] the Jikeikai in 1917,[313] and the Chiho Shikokukai in 1928,[314] in an attempt to unify thought according to national policy. And he played a leading role in the emperor's awarding Nichiren the honorary title "Great Teacher for Establishing the Truth"[315] in 1922.

Senoo felt dissatisfied with the lack of spirit in established Buddhist groups, and in 1919 with some colleagues he established the Great Japanese Nichiren Youth Group,[316] which leapt into vigorous, practical action. At that time the group had a nationalistic color but was based on a kind of humanism, using such slogans as "faith and love." Its core members were youth from farming villages. Later, having directly witnessed a succession of economic crises, labor disputes, and tenant farmer disputes, Senoo's social concern intensified. Sometimes he was so involved in solving tenant farmer disputes that he was revered as greatly as Nichiren is now.

According to his own recollections, he realized, through being involved in these disputes, that idealistic lectures and sermons removed from actual life only benefitted landlords and capitalists, and that mediation that merely sought to persuade landlords and comfort the proletariat was not in accord with the Buddha's intention. When the Showa period arrived, he gradually grew critical of the system of monopolistic capitalism, insisting that such a system was against the egalitarian spirit of Buddhism. He wanted to overthrow it.

In 1931, Senoo, splitting from some of his comrades who disagreed with his views, once again organized the Emerging Buddhist Youth League.[317] When the League was formed, he put forth three basic principles: proclaiming reverence for Shakyamuni Buddha, establishing the buddha-land of faith and love on earth, and correcting the capitalistic system, which is contrary to the spirit of Buddhism and obstructs the welfare of the people. He began to criticize the Japanese imperial system and to consider its overthrow. He says that he was stimulated by books by Lenin, such as *The State and Revolution* (1917), and that he found his spiritual support in Nichiren's criticism of monarchy as seen in his *Admonition with Hachiman*.[318]

Senoo opposed materialism based on a Buddhist idea of unity of mind and matter, but he accepted the idea of violent revolution as an exceptional means for speedily realizing the buddha-land on earth, and he was willing to entertain the idea that a temporary dictatorship of the proletariat was permissible. He also used internationalism as a slogan. He picked up on Nichiren's view of the Mongolian invasion as punishment of Japan by saints from a neighboring country. He pointed to this as a model of internationalism and therefore thought it blasphemous to set Nichiren up as a nationalist. He also thought that the sangha during the time of Shakyamuni was a cooperative community with common property and that fundamental Buddhist teachings such as selflessness, emptiness, interdependent relations, interdependent origination, and so forth, implied the socialist ideal of community.

Citing the phrase "the innumerable meanings emerge from one Dharma," drawn from the second chapter of the Sutra of Innumerable Meanings—regarded as the opening or introductory sutra to the Lotus Sutra—he insisted that Buddhism should always develop in accord with the times and society, and he asked the established Buddhist groups to reflect on their inflexible attitudes.

Senoo turned a critical eye not only toward established Nichiren sects but toward established Nichirenism, which was determinedly nationalistic. When he established the Alliance of New Buddhist Youth, he moved away from Nichirenism as it had been up to then, and began to take a pan-Buddhist stance. Yet he did not deny Nichiren's relevance, which we know from the fact that he occasionally cited Nichiren. What he discarded in trying to bring life to Nichiren for the coming age was the thick shell that later generations had put around Nichiren. For the April 1931 issue of *Under the Flag of New Buddhism* (later just *New Buddhism*), the Alliance's bulletin, he wrote an essay entitled "Turn toward New Buddhist Youth," in which he said, "I threw off Saint Nichiren's old coat, in an attempt to restore his spirit to the contemporary world."

Moreover, as indicated earlier, while maintaining the unity of mind and matter against materialism, Senoo also criticized the spiritualism of the newly emerging Buddhist movements as nothing more than idealistic adaptations of established Buddhism. As an example he pointed to the "Truth Movement"[319] of Entei Tomomatsu.[320]

Senoo was active in the proletariat liberation movement, labor unions, and labor disputes. As a result, the government's oppressive power finally caught up with him, and in November of 1936 he was arrested and the Alliance of New Buddhist Youth forced to dissolve. But after the War he took part in the peace movement with his comrades.

Government oppression was not only directed against socialist political activities but toward anything that did not go along with the nationalism of absolute imperial power. As a result, incidents of oppression and imprisonment occurred among Christians and Buddhists and even among the new religious movements.

Among the new religious movements, the oppression of Omoto-kyo[321] was the most violent. New religions were often oppressed when they were getting started. At that time they were controlled by strict government regulations, with the excuse that they were dedicated to false and obscene gods. The fact that they were people-centered or interested in social reform sometimes led to antiauthoritarian speech and behavior among the new religious movements. Because of this they were frequently charged with the crime of disrespecting the emperor.

Because of its universality as a world religion, and its occasionally progressive thought and movements, Christianity became an object of oppression, too. In general, established Buddhists adapted themselves to the will of the government, and those parts of the writings of their founders and others that were examined and found to be undesirable had to be purged. For example, in 1939 the authorities examined Shinran's words "Everyone, from lords to subjects, goes against the Dharma and fails to do what is right," which appear in a chapter of Shinran's *Teaching, Practice, Faith, and Realization*,[322] and that part of the book had to be deleted. In Nichiren's case, several hundred passages had to be deleted as disrespectful. In Nichiren's writings, the authority of the Buddha and the Buddha-dharma are held high, below which come the authority of gods, emperors, and nations. There were a number of places where his words were examined, criticized, and had to be deleted on account of being disrespectful.

Furthermore, some of Nichiren's followers were imprisoned for such crimes of disrespect toward the emperor. They were not ideologically believers in socialism and the like, but simply accepted the words of Nichiren as they were. For that they were thrown in prison. Tsunesaburo Makiguchi,[323] the first president of Soka Gakkai, for example, was arrested and put in prison, as were the second president, Josei Toda,[324] and twenty other leaders in 1943. Makiguchi died in prison. Toda was released only at the end of the War. Their arrests were made in connection with Ise Shrine talismans.

At that time the government set up Shinto shrines as part of the system of State Shinto. As a way of controlling various religions, every religious group was forced to accept talismans from the Ise Shrine. But Soka Gakkai refused. This is why it was suppressed and its leaders imprisoned. Their refusal originated from Nichiren's idea that the good gods had abandoned the country and had returned to the heavenly realm. Nichiren had taught that the Japanese gods had been converted to the Buddha-dharma and had become good guardian deities of the Dharma. But since there was no longer any true Dharma in Japan, they had abandoned Japan and gone to the heavenly realm. Accordingly, there are no gods in the Shinto shrines, and it is a waste of time to visit them. The talismans are empty of value. They are nothing more than plain pieces of paper. Thus, the Nichiren sects developed the idea of refusing to pray at Shinto shrines.

In True Pure Land (*shinshu*) Buddhism the same idea arose from a different perspective. There, Buddha-dharma means the *nembutsu*—chanting praise to Amida Buddha—and the guardian deities are pleased so long as the *nembutsu* is recited. So there is no need to visit Shinto shrines other than for the purpose of reciting the *nembutsu*. Thus, during the Tokugawa period, scholars of the school of National Learning such as Atsutane Hirata attacked the Nichiren and True Pure Land schools as enemies of the gods.[325]

This is why Makiguchi and others refused to accept the talismans from Ise Shrine. Since the gods had returned to the heavenly realm and were no longer at the shrines, the talismans were meaningless. Makiguchi and the others had no political ideology for resisting state power. But they did engage in passive resistance, and for this they were imprisoned.

Other incidents of suppression and imprisonment regarding the mandala of ten realms occurred in the Eight-chapter Faction of the Main Gate School[326] of the Lotus Sect. The mandala of ten realms is a scroll in which representatives of each of the ten realms of existence[327] were inscribed around the *daimoku*[328] in the center. The names of the Shinto gods Amaterasu—the Sun Goddess—and Great Bodhisattva Hachiman were written under the *daimoku*. Government authorities attacked this, claiming that Amaterasu was being kicked by the *daimoku*. Nichiryu (1385–1464),[329] the founder of the Main Gate School, had placed Amaterasu and other gods in the realms of hungry spirits and beasts. This was quoted in a textbook used in the Main Gate School seminary. When the Ministry of Education saw this in 1941, several of the sect's leaders were arrested for the crime of disrespecting the emperor. One died in prison and the rest were released under the postwar abolition of the crime of disrespecting the emperor.

This incident, too, did not happen as a consequence of having an anti-authoritarian or revolutionary ideology. It was an unintentional demonstration of the fact that, from the point of view of the authorities, there is something dangerous in the thought of Nichiren.

We have now discussed Nichiren and some of his followers. Such things are very interesting and their further examination and analysis would be very valuable.

Notes

1. Yoshio Tamura, *Hokke-kyō: shinri, seimei, jissen* 法華経：真理・生命・実践 (Tokyo: Chūō Kōron Sha, 1969 and 1991).

2. *hongaku shisō* 本覺思想, also translated as the thought or idea of "originary," "inherent," or "innate" enlightenment.

3. The most relevant literature in English includes: Jacqueline I. Stone, *Original Enlightenment and the Transformation of Medieval Japanese Buddhism* (Honolulu: University of Hawaii, 1999); the special issue of the *Japanese Journal of Religious Studies* on Tendai Buddhism in Japan edited by Paul Swanson (*Japanese Journal of Religious Studies* 14, nos. 2–3 [1987]), which includes Tamura's "Japanese Culture and the Tendai Concept of Original Enlightenment"; the "mini-special" issue of the same journal, which includes four articles on *hongaku shisō* (*Japanese Journal of Religious Studies* 22, nos. 1–2 [1995]); and *Pruning the Bodhi Tree: The Storm over Critical Buddhism*, edited by Jamie Hubbard and Paul L. Swanson (Honolulu: University of Hawaii, 1997).

4. The most relevant text for pursuing this matter is Tamura's *Hongaku Shisō Ron* 本覚思想論 [Essays on Original Enlightenment Thought] (Tokyo: Shunjūsha, 1990).

5. Chigaku Tanaka (1861–1939), Ikki Kita (1883–1937), Chogyū Takayama (1871–1902), Kenji Miyazawa (1896–1933), and Hotsumi Ozaki (1901–44).

6. *wanshan tong gui jiao (monzen-dōki-kyō)* 万善同帰教. Literally, "the teaching that unifies all that is good."

7. Chih-i 智顗.

8. T'ien-t'ai (Tendai) 天台.

9. *Shōbōgenzō* 正法眼蔵.

10. Zhongguo 中国.

11. 姉崎正治.

12. Masaharu Anesaki, *Genshinbutsu to hosshinbutsu* 現身仏と法身仏 (Tōkyō: Yūhōkan, 1901).

13. Masaharu Anesaki, *Konpon bukkyo* 根本仏教 (Tōkyō: Hakubunkan, 1910).

14. 富永仲基. The Western practice of placing the family name last is followed here and throughout this book. However, like other Japanese scholars, we have followed Tamura's practice of referring to many earlier scholars by their given names. Thus Nakamoto Tominaga is referred to as "Nakamoto" despite the fact that Nakamoto is his given name.

15. *Shutsujō Kōgo* 出定後語, originally published in two volumes in 1745. The work has been republished recently as Nakamoto Tominaga, *Chūkai Shutsujō Kōgo* 注解出定後語 (Tōkyō: Ōzorasha, 1996).

16. Nakamoto Tominaga, *Emerging from Meditation*, trans. Michael Pye (London: Duckworth, 1990), 168.

17. Āgama sūtras; *Agon* 阿含. A northern equivalent of the Pāli Nikāyas, or the Pāli Canon, preserved primarily in Chinese, now mostly lost in Sanskrit.

18. Tominaga, *Emerging from Meditation*, 120–124. Pye translates *gen'ari sanbutsu* 言有三部 as "Language has three conditions."

19. Hattori Ten'yū (i.e., Somon) 服部天遊.

20. Hattori Ten'yū, *Sekirara* 赤裸々 (Tōkyō: Tōhō Shoin, [between 1930 and 1931]).

21. Hirata Atsutane 平田篤胤.

22. Atsutane Hirata, *Shutsujō Shōgo* 出定笑語 ([Japan, s.l.], 1849).

23. Norinaga Motoori, *Tamakatsuma* 玉勝間 (Tōkyō: Iwanami Shoten, 1934).

24. *genshi kyōten* 原始教典.

25. *genshi bukkyō* 原始仏教.

26. Nakamoto Tominaga and Hattori Ten'yū, *Gappon Shitsujō Kōgō Sekirara* 合本 出定後語 赤裸々 [*Emerging from Meditation* and *Nakedness* in One Volume] (Tokyo: Komei-sha, 1902), 82.

27. Murakami Senjō 村上専精.

28. Murakami Senjō, *Bukkyō Tōitsuron* 仏教統一論 (Tōkyō: Shoshishinsui, 2011).

29. Gene Reeves, trans., *The Lotus Sutra* (Boston: Wisdom, 2008), 141.

30. *śūnyatā*; *kū* 空.

31. *kūmu* 空無.

32. *komu* 虚無.

33. This passage is found in the Madhyama Āgama (Chū-agon 中阿含), 22. Adapted here from Bhikkhu Bodhi's translation of a parallel version (*Alagaddūpama Sutta*) that exists in Pāli: *The Middle Length Discourses of the Buddha: A Translation of the Majjhima Nikāya*, trans. Bhikkhu Bodhi (Boston: Wisdom, 1995), 234.

34. Saṃyukta Āgama (Zō-agon 雑阿含), 12 and 15. A parallel version is found in the Pāli Nikāyas at Saṃyutta Nikāya II:15, Kaccānagotta Sutta.

35. Adapted here from *The Connected Discourses of the Buddha: A Translation of the Saṃyutta Nikāya*, trans. Bhikkhu Bodhi (Boston: Wisdom, 2000), 544.

36. Reeves, *The Lotus Sutra*, 90.

37. Skt.: *ākāśa*; Jap.: *koku* 虚空.

38. Mahā-prajñāparamitā Sūtra; Maka-hannyaharamitta-shingyō 摩訶般若波羅蜜多經. Adapted here from *The Large Sutra on Perfect Wisdom*, trans. Edward Conze (Berkeley: University of California, 1975), 100.

39. Ibid: chapter 82.

40. Vimalakīrti-nirdeśa Sūtra; Yuimakitsu shosetsu kyō 維摩詰所説經.

41. *The Vimalakīrti Sutra*, trans. John McRae (Berkeley: Numata Center for Buddhist Translation and Research, 2004), 145.

42. Prajña-hṛdaya-paramitā Sūtra; Hannya shingyō 般若心経.

43. *Mahāprajñāparāmitā-upadeśa-śāstra; Daichido-ron* 大智度論. The Sanskrit title is a conjecture based on Kumarajiva's Chinese translation. No Sanskrit text has been found.

44. Nāgârjuna; Lóngshù, Ryūju 龍樹.

45. Mūlamadhyamakakārikā; Zhōnglùn, Chūron 中論.

46. Mark Siderits and Shōryū Katsura, *Nāgārjuna's Middle Way: Mūlamadhyamakakārikā* (Boston: Wisdom, 2013), 276.

47. 湛然, Tannen in Japanese pronunciation.

48. *tathāgata*; *rúlái, nyorai* 如来. Often interpreted in English as "thus-come."

49. *nyo* 如.

50. *shinnyo* 真如.

51. Avataṃsaka Sūtra; Huáyán jīng, Kegon-gyō 華嚴經.

52. Dvādaśanikāya-śāstra; Jūnimon-ron 十二門論.

53. Āryadeva 聖提婆 Shōdaiba in Japanese. His exact dates are not known.

54. Śata-śāstra; Hyaku-ron 百論.

55. Catuḥśataka-śāstra; Yonhyaku-ron 四百論.

56. 三論 Sānlùn, Sanron. The Three Treatise School (三論宗) is basically the Chinese version of Indian *Madhyamaka*.

57. 四論宗 Sìlùn zōng, Shiron shū. This sect, established in the Northern Wei, was a branch of the Sānlùn sect.

58. Tathāgata-garbha Sūtra (Daihōkō-nyorai-zō-kyō 大方廣如來藏經); Anūnatvāpūrṇatva-nirdeśa Sūtra (Bussetsu fusōfugen kyō 佛說不增不減經); Aṅgulimāla Sūtra (Ōkutsumara-kyō 央掘摩羅經); Śrīmālādevī-siṃha-nāda Sūtra (Shōman-gyō 勝鬘經); Mahāparinirvāṇa Sūtra (Dai nehan-gyō 大涅槃經); and Anuttarāśraya Sūtra (Mujōe-kyō 無上依經).

59. *ālaya-vijñāna*; *araya-shiki* 阿黎耶識.

60. Saṃdhi-nirmocana Sūtra (Gejinmikkyō 解深密經) and Māhāyāna-abhidharma Sūtra (Abidatsuma-daijō-kyō 阿毘達磨大乘經).

61. Yogâcāra ; Vijñapti-mātra; Yuishiki 唯識.

62. The Mahāyāna-saṃgraha-śāstra (Shō-ron 攝論), Prakaraṇārya-vāca śāstra (Kenyō shōgyō ron 顯揚聖教論), and Abidharma-samuccaya (Abidatsumashū-ron 阿毘達磨集論).

63. The Viṃśatikā (Nijū-ron 二十論), Triṃśikā (Sanjū-ron 三十論), Buddhagotra śāstra (Busshō-ron 佛性論), and Mahāyāna-saṃgraha-bhāṣya (Shōdaijō-ron-seishin-shaku 攝大乘論世親釋).

64. 法華経論 Hokekyō-ron.

65. Laṅkāvatāra Sūtra (Ryōga-kyō 楞伽經) and Mahā-ghanavyūha Sūtra (Daijō-mitsugon kyō 大乘密嚴經).

66. Mahāvairocana Sūtra (Dainichi-kyō 大日經) and Vajraśekhara Sūtra (Kongōchō-kyō 金剛頂經).

67. Though Tamura refers to the twenty-seven chapter Sanskrit version, in this book all chapter references are to the twenty-eight chapter version that is used for all translations from Chinese into English.

68. *bosatsu* 菩薩.

69. *kakuujō* 覚有情.

70. Prabhūtaratna; Tahō 多宝.

71. Viśiṣṭacāritra; Jōgyō 上行.

72. Reeves, *The Lotus Sutra*, 289. References to this translation are for the convenience of the reader. Typically, Tamura translated into Japanese from Sanskrit, which is often at variance with the Chinese version, which is the version from which almost all English versions have been translated.

73. Watson's translation has: "Free of worldly attachments, like the lotus blossom, constantly you move within the realm of emptiness and quiet" (*The Vimalakirti Sutra*, trans. Burton Watson [New York: Columbia University, 1997], 25).

74. The Taoist term *wu wei* (*mui*) 無為.

75. Watson, *The Vimilakirti Sutra*, 95: "The lotus does not grow on the upland plain; the lotus grows in the mud and mire of a damp low-lying place. . . . It is only when living beings are in the midst of the mire of earthly desires that they turn to the Buddha Law."

76. Reeves, *The Lotus Sutra*, 293.

77. Sadāparibhūta; Jōbikyōman 常被輕慢.

78. Shō-hokke-kyō 正法華経.

79. Dharmarakṣa 法護, often written 竺法護.

80. Myōhō-renge-kyō 妙法蓮華經.

81. Kumārajīva; Kumarajū 鳩摩羅什.

82. Tenbon-myōhō-renge-kyō 添品妙法蓮華經.

83. Jñānagupta; Janakutta 闍那崛多 and Dharmagupta; Darumagyūta 達摩笈多.

84. 南条文雄.

85. The standard script for writing Hindi and most other Indian languages.

86. Unrai Ogiwara and Katsuya Tsuchida, *Saddharmapuṇḍarīka-sūtram: Romanized and Revised Text of the Bibliotheca Buddhica Publication by Consulting a Skt. Ms. and Tibetan and Chinese Translations* (Tokyo: Seigo-Kenkyūka, 1934–35).

87. H. Kern, *Saddharma-Puṇḍarīka or The Lotus of the True Law*, Sacred Books of the East, 21 (Oxford: Clarendon, 1884, 1909). Also New York: Dover, 1963.

88. E. Burnouf, *Le Lotus de la Bonne Loi*, 2 vols. (Paris: Imprimerie Nationale, 1844 and 1852; new edition, 1925).

89. Ekai Kawaguchi, *Bonzōdenyaku-myōhō-byaku-renge-kyō* 梵蔵伝訳妙法白蓮華経 (Tōkyō: Sekai Bunko Kankōkai, 1924).

90. Izumi Hōkei 泉芳璟.

91. Nanjio Bunyiu, *Bonkan Taishō Shinyaku Hokekkyō* 梵漢對照新譯法華經 (Kyoto: Jingenkai Shuppanbu, 1913). Translated into modern Japanese by Y. Iwamoto and Yukio Sakamoto, *Hokekyō* 法華経, 3 vols. (Tokyo: Iwanami Shoten, 1962, 1976, 1989).

92. Kyōsui Oka, *Bonbun Wayaku Hokekkyō* 梵文和訳法華経 (Ōsaka: Yagō Shoten, 1924).

93. The following translations into English from Kumarajiva's Chinese translation are currently available:

The Threefold Lotus Sutra: Innumerable Meanings, The Lotus Flower of the Wonderful Law, and Meditation on the Bodhisattva Universal Virtue, Bunnō Katō, trans., rev. W. E. Soothill and Wilhelm Schiffer (Tokyo: Kosei, 1971 and 1975).

Scripture of the Lotus Blossom of the Fine Dharma (The Lotus Sūtra), rev. ed., trans. Leon Hurvitz (New York: Columbia University, 2009).

The Wonderful Dharma Lotus Flower Sutra, with commentary by Tripitaka Master Hua, 10 vols., The Buddhist Text Translation Society (San Francisco: Sino-American Buddhist Association, 1976–82).

The Lotus Sutra: The Sutra of the Lotus Flower of the Wonderful Dharma, trans. Senchū Murano (Tokyo: Nichiren Shu Shimbun, 1974 and 1991).

The Lotus Sutra: The White Lotus of the Marvelous Law, rev. ed., trans. Tsugunari Kubo and Akira Yuyama (Tokyo and Berkeley: Bukkyō Dendō Kyōkai and Numata Center for Buddhist Translation and Research, 2007).

The Lotus Sutra: A Contemporary Translation of a Buddhist Classic, trans. Gene Reeves (Boston: Wisdom, 2008).

The Lotus Sutra, trans. Burton Watson (New York: Columbia University, 1993).

The Lotus Sutra and Its Opening and Closing Sutras, trans. Burton Watson (Tokyo: Soka Gakkai, 2009).

94. Tominaga, *Emerging from Meditation*, 168 and 170.

95. Tominaga and Hattori, *Gappon Shutsujō Kōgō Sekirara* 合本 出定後語赤裸々.

96. *Fahua xuanyi (Hokke-gengi)* 法華玄義, chapter 10, first section.

97. Tominaga, *Emerging from Meditation*, 169.

98. Third section of *Shitsujō shōgo* 出定笑語.

99. Reeves, *The Lotus Sutra*, 235.

100. 堅意 (Sthiramati, also translated as 安慧 An'ne), 入大乗論 Nyūdaijōron.

101. *kaihui* 開會.

102. Tamura discusses Tendai thought at greater length in "Japanese Culture and the Tendai Concept of Original Enlightenment," *Japanese Journal of Religious Studies* 14:2–3 (June–September 1987) 203–10, and in "Tendai Philosophy: The Ideal and the Real," chapter 6 of his *Japanese Buddhism: A Cultural History* (Tokyo: Kosei, 2000).

103. *Tama no ogushi* 玉の小櫛 (literally, a jewel's small comb). See *Motoori Norinaga Zenshū* 本居宣長全集 [The Complete Works of Norinaga Motoori], vol. 4 (Tōkyō: Chikuma Shobō, 1968–93).

104. *Korai fūtei-shō* 古来風体抄. A translation of a key section of this text and a discussion of the relation of Shunzei's and Teika's poetry to the Lotus Sutra can be found in William R. LaFleur, "Symbol and Yūgen: Shunzei's Use of Tendai Buddhism," chapter 4 of his *The Karma of Words: Buddhism and the Literary Arts in Medieval Japan* (Berkeley: University of California Press, 1983), 80–106.

105. 吉田兼俱.

106. *yuiitsu shintō* 唯一神道.

107. 白隠慧鶴.

108. "*Ōrategama* 遠羅天釜," found in *Hakuin-osho Zenshu* 白隠和尚全集 [The Collected Works of Abbot Hakuin], vol. 5 (Tōkyō: Ryugin-sha, 1934), 18–22.

109. 道生 Dōshō in Japanese pronunciation.

110. Translated in: Young-Ho Kim, *Tao-sheng's Commentary on the Lotus Sūtra* (Albany: State University of New York, 1990).

111. Kim, *Tao-sheng's Commentary on the Lotus Sūtra*, 162.

112. 法雲 Hōun in Japanese pronunciation.

113. *Fahua jing yi ji (Hokke-gengi-ki)* 法華経義記.

114. 如是 *nyoze*.

115. Reeves, *The Lotus Sutra*, 83–84.

116. Ibid., 88.

117. Ibid., 96.

118. *upāya-kauśalya*; *ōwakushara* 傴和拘舍羅. For an extended discussion of this term, see: Michael Pye, *Skillful Means* (London: Duckworth, 1978).

119. Reeves, *The Lotus Sutra*, 126–27.

120. Ibid., 141.

121. Ibid., 161. More literally, "of one character and flavor."

122. Ibid., 160.

123. Ibid., 164.

124. Ibid., 165.

125. Ibid., 160.

126. Ibid., 224.

127. Ibid., 231.

128. Ibid., 246.

129. *sokushinjōbutsu* 即身成仏.

130. In chapter 8 of his *Fahua wenju ji* (*Hokke-mongu-ki*) 法華文句記, a commentary on Tiantai Zhiyi's *Fahua wenju* (*Hokke-mongu*) 法華文句 [Words and Phrases of the Lotus Sutra].

131. The relation of chapter 12 to the sutra as a whole is quite complicated. In some early versions, including Dharmaraksha's translation of 286 CE, it is included as a part of the previous chapter, in others it is given as a separate chapter, and in still others it does not appear at all. Apparently it was not included in Kumarajiva's original translation, though this has been much debated in East Asia.

132. Reeves, *The Lotus Sutra*, 257–60.

133. Ibid., 265.

134. Ibid., 262.

135. Viśiṣṭacāritra (Jōgyō 上行), Anantācāritra (Muhengyō 無辺行), Viśuddhacāritra (Jōgyō 浄行), and Supratiṣṭhitacāritra (Anryūgyō 安立行).

136. Reeves, *The Lotus Sutra*, 289.

137. Ibid., 291–92.

138. Ibid.

139. H. Kern, trans., *Saddharma-Puṇḍarīka: or, The Lotus of the True Law* (New York: Dover, 1963), 310, 307, and 308.

140. J. A. B. van Buitenen, trans., *The Bhagavadgītā in the Mahābhārata: Text and Translation* (Chicago: University of Chicago Press, 1981) 87, 107, and 121 (verses 4:6, 9:17, and 12:7). Kern quotes only the Sanskrit.

141. Kern, *Saddharma-Puṇḍarīka*, 124.

142. van Buitenen, *The Bhagavadgītā in the Mahābhārata*, 107.

143. Here Tamura follows the Sanskrit version, which differs from the Chinese. See Leon Hurvitz, *Scripture of the Lotus Blossom of the Fine Dharma (The Lotus Sūtra)*, 357.

144. Kern, *Saddharma-Puṇḍarīka*, 368.

145. van Buitenen, *The Bhagavadgītā in the Mahābhārata*, 117.

146. *śraddhā*; *shin* 信.

147. *adhimukti*; *shinge* 信解.

148. *prasāda*; *chōjō* 澄浄.

149. *rūpakāya*; *nikushin* 肉身 (*shikishin* 色身, *shōshin* 生身, and *genshin* 現身 are also used in Japanese).

150. *dharmakāya*; *hōshin* 法身.

151. *nirmāṇakāya*; *ōjin* 応身 or 應身.

152. *sambhogakāya*; *hōshin* 報身 Also translated as "the body of bliss" and as "the enjoyment body." It is the body in which the blissful rewards of awakening are enjoyed.

153. Avalokiteśvara; Kanzeon 觀世音.

154. Reeves, *The Lotus Sutra*, 293.

155. Ibid., 296.

156. Ibid.

157. Ibid., 237–39.

158. Ibid., 297.

159. Ibid., 308.

160. Ibid., 95.

161. Ibid., 333.

162. Translated from Sanskrit.

163. Reeves, *The Lotus Sutra*, 338.

164. *shakubuku* 折伏 Literally "bend and subdue."

165. Reeves, *The Lotus Sutra*, 346-47.

166. Ibid., 347.

167. *parinirvāṇa* 般涅槃 *hatsu nehan*.

168. Myōhō-renge-kyō-an 妙法蓮華経庵.

169. Reeves, *The Lotus Sutra*, 349.

170. *ājñā* or *preṣaṇa*; *chokumei* 勅命 in Japanese.

171. Reeves, *The Lotus Sutra*, 352.

172. *shōshinjisatsu* 焼身供養.

173. Reeves, *The Lotus Sutra*, 359.

174. Ibid., 360.

175. Ibid.

176. *fushakushinmyō* 不惜身命.

177. *Taihō-ritsuryō* 大宝律令 (701 CE).

178. *semuisha* 施無畏者.

179. *sōji* 総持.

180. *nōji* 能持.

181. *nōsha* 能遮.

182. Hārītī; 鬼子母神; Guǐzǐmǔshénin in Chinese, Kishimojin or Kishibojin in Japanese.

183. In some versions of this story she feeds the children of others to her own children.

184. Reeves, *The Lotus Sutra*, 386.

185. Ibid., 389.

186. Kan-fugen-bosatsu-gyōbō-kyō 観普賢菩薩行法経.

187. *jissōzange* 実相懺悔.

188. Reeves, *The Lotus Sutra*, 419.

189. Ibid., 416.

190. Ibid., 417.

191. Ibid., 416. *muzaisōzange* 無罪相懺悔.

192. Ibid., 240.

193. Ibid., 293.

194. 法雲.

195. In the first volume of *Fahua xuanyi* (*Hokke-gengi*) 法華玄義.

196. Nichiren, "The Third Doctrine," in *The Major Writings of Nichiren Daishonin*, rev. ed., vol. 7 (Tokyo: Nichiren Shoshu International Center, 1994), 129–35.

197. Nichiren, "Risshō Ankoku Ron," in *The Major Writings of Nichiren Daishonin*, rev. ed., vol. 2 (Tokyo: Nichiren Shoshu International Center, 1995), 3–46.

198. Nichiren, "Kyōkijikoku Shō," in *The Major Writings of Nichiren Daishonin*, vol. 4 (Tokyo: Nichiren Shoshu International Center, 1986), 7–21.

199. Nichiren, "Kenhōbō Shō," in *The Major Writings of Nichiren Daishonin*, vol. 1 (Tokyo: Nichiren Shoshu International Center, 1979), 163–68.

200. Nichiren, "Kaimoku Shō," *The Major Writings of Nichiren Daishonin*, rev. ed., vol. 2 (Tokyo: Nichiren Shoshu International Center, 1995), 59–188.

201. Nichiren, "Kanjin Honzon Shō," *The Major Writings of Nichiren Daishonin*, vol. 1 (Tokyo: Nichiren Shoshu International Center, 1979), 45–83.

202. *wu (mu)* 無.

203. 僧肇, *Sōjō* in Japanese.

204. *Zhaolun (Chōron)* 肇論. See: Walter Liebenthal, *The Treatise of Chao* (Hong Kong: Hong Kong University, 1968).

205. *Fahua xuanyi (Hokke-gengi)* 法華玄義 For an extensive discussion and partial translation, see: Paul L. Swanson, *T'ien-T'ai Philosophy* (Berkeley: Asian Humanities Press, 1989).

206. *Miaofa lianhua jing yishu (Myōhō-renge-kyō-gisho)* 妙法蓮華経義疏. See: Kim, *Tao-sheng's Commentary on the Lotus Sūtra*.

207. *Lianhua jing yiji (Renge-kyō-giki)* 蓮華経義記.

208. 会前開後.

209. Kim, *Tao-sheng's Commentary on the Lotus Sūtra*, 78.

210. *Fahua wenju (Hokke-mongu)* 法華文句. The full title is *Miaofa lianhua jing wenju (Myōhō-renge-kyō-mongu)* 妙法蓮華經文句.

211. *Fahua xuanyi (Hokke-gengi)* 法華玄義.

212. *Mohe zhiguan (Maka-shikan)* 魔訶止観 For a study and translation of the first chapter, see: Neal Donner & Daniel B. Stevenson, *The Great Calming and Contemplation* (Honolulu: University of Hawaii, 1993).

213. 灌頂 Kanjō, also known as 章安 Zhang'an, Shōan.

214. First part of the second fascicle.

215. Ibid.

216. *jue dai miao (zettaimyō)* 絶待妙.

217. *juedui dejuedui (zettaiteki zettai)* 絶対的絶対.

218. First part of the second fascicle of *Fahua xuanyi (Hokke-gengi)* 法華玄義.

219. Ibid.

220. Siderits and Katsura, *Nāgārjuna's Middle Way*, 277. For a variety of translations of this famous verse and a discussion of it, see: Swanson, *Foundations of T'ien-T'ai Philosophy*, 3.

221. *Pusa yingluo benye jing (Bosatsu-yōraku-hongō-kyō)* 菩薩瓔珞本業経. Often referred to simply as the *Yingluo jing (Yōraku-kyō)* 瓔珞経, it and its influence on Zhiyi are discussed in chapter 3 of Swanson's *Foundations of T'ien-T'ai Philosophy*.

222. 湛燃 Zhanran (711–82) Also known as *Miaole Dashi Zhanran* 妙樂大師湛然 and *Jingqi* 荊溪. If Tiantai Zhiyi is counted as its founder, Zhanran is the sixth patriarch of Tiantai, but, if as is sometimes done, the lineage is traced back to Nagarjuna, Zhanran is the twelfth patriarch.

223. First part of the seventh fascicle of *Fahua xuanyi (Hokke-gengi)* 法華玄義.

224. Last part of the ninth fascicle of *Fahua wenju (Hokke-mongu)* 法華文句.

225. First part of the fifth fascicle of *Mohe zhiguan (Maka-shikan)* 魔訶止観.

226. Ibid.

227. Ibid.

228. *Guanyin xuanyi (Kannon-gengi)* 観音玄義.

229. *Fahua xuanyi (Hokke-gengi)* 法華玄義. Last part of the fifth fascicle.

230. First part of the eighth fascicle. For a more recent, more extensive, and somewhat different discussion of good and evil in Tiantai thought, see Brook Ziporyn, *Evil and/or/ as The Good: Omnicentrism, Intersubjectivity, and Value Paradox in Tiantai Buddhist Thought* (Cambridge: Harvard University Asia Center, 2000)

231. 灌頂, 智威, 慧威 and 玄朗.

232. Zhanran 妙樂.
233. 澄觀 Chōkan in Japanese.
234. 知礼, also known as Siming Zhili 四明知礼.
235. *Shanjia (Sange)* 山家.
236. *Shanwai (Sangai)* 山外.
237. Avataṃsaka Sūtra; Huayan jing (Kegon-kyō) 華嚴經. The title is frequently translated as the "Flower Ornament Sutra."
238. Dengyō Daishi Saichō 傳教大師最澄. For a more recent account of Saicho's life and work, see Paul Groner, *Saicho: The Establishment of the Japanese Tendai School* (Berkeley: Asian Humanities Press, 1984).
239. 道邃, the seventh patriarch of the Tiantai school, and 行滿.
240. *hongaku* 本覺.
241. *mappō* 末法.
242. 法然 Hōnen, founder of the Pure Land school in Japan.
243. 親鸞, 道元, 日蓮.
244. *Jōkyū no Ran* 丞久の乱.
245. Hojō 北条.
246. *Risshō ankoku ron* 立正安國論.
247. Nichizō 日像.
248. *Nichiren-shū* 日蓮宗 also known as the *Hokke-shū* 法華宗.
249. Myōken-ji 妙顕寺.
250. Nichijū 日什.
251. Myōman-ji 妙満寺.
252. Jōdo-shin-shū 淨土眞宗, founded by Shinran, often referred to simply as Shin-shū 眞宗.
253. *Monto Koji* 門徒古事.
254. *Tenmon Hokke no Ran* 天文法華の乱.
255. *shōen* 荘園.
256. *dogō* 土豪.
257. 蓮如.
258. 本願寺. Now Nishi-Honganji 西本願寺.
259. *Ikkō ikki* 一向一揆 Literally, single-minded rebellion.
260. *Fuju-fuse-ha* 不受不施派.
261. *shakubuku* 折伏.
262. 日仁 and 日実.
263. 日親.
264. Nakayama-monryū 中山門流.
265. Nikkyō 日経.
266. Jōraku-in 常楽院.
267. Keichō Hōnan 慶長法難.
268. Hōkō-ji 方広寺.
269. Nichiō 日奥.
270. Myōkaku-ji 妙覚寺.
271. Hokkeshū Kanjō 法華宗諫状.
272. 対馬 An island approximately midway between Kyushu and the Korean peninsula.
273. 日閑.
274. Myōgaku-in 妙覚院.

275. 日勢.

276. *Tenpō Hōnan* 天保法難.

277. 田中智学.

278. *Kokuchū-kai* 国柱会.

279. 北一輝.

280. *Kokutairon oyobi junsei shakaishugi* 国体論及び純正社会主義.

281. *Shina kakumei gaishi* 支那革命外史.

282. 石原莞爾 His family name is often Anglicized as Ishiwara.

283. Ishihara Kanji, *Sensōshi taikan no yurai ki* 戦争史大観の由来記. (Tokyo: Chuokoron-Sha, 1941).

284. Takayama Chogyū 高山樗牛.

285. *Shūmon no Ishin* 宗門之維新 (Shishiō-bunko, 1897).

286. Chogyū Takayama, *Nichiren shōnin to Nihonkoku* 日蓮上人と日本国 [Saint Nichiren and the Nation of Japan] in Chogyū Collected Works 樗牛全集 (Tokyo: Hakubunkan Shinsha, 1904).

287. 宮沢賢治.

288. Daitō Shimaji, *Myōhō-renge-kyō: kanwa taishō* 妙法蓮華経：漢和対照 [The Lotus Sutra in Chinese and Japanese] (Tōkyō: Meiji Shoin, 1921).

289. Shimaji Daitō 島地大等.

290. Miyazawa Kenji, *Nōmin geijutsu gairon kōyō* 農民芸術概論綱要 [An Outline Survey of Farmers' Art] in Miyazawa Kenji Collected Works, vol. 10 宮沢賢治全集１０ (Tokyo: Chikumashobo, 1995), 18–26. Ironically, while virtually nothing of Miyazawa's was published during his lifetime, since then several of his collected works have appeared in which most of what he wrote can now be found.

291. For assistance with and often the actual wording of the translations of the Miyazawa poems on this and the following pages we are much indebted to Hiroaki Sato, translator of: *Spring & Asura: Poems of Kenji Miyazawa* (Chicago: Chicago Review, 1973), Miyazawa Kenji, *A Future of Ice: Poems and Stories of a Japanese Buddhist* (San Francisco: North Point, 1989), and *Miyazawa Kenji: Selections* (University of California, 2007).

292. Miyazawa would have known April 28 as the day of the founding of the Nichiren School, based on the legend that at sunrise on that day while facing the Pacific Ocean from Mt. Kiyozumi, Nichiren started chanting *Namu myōhō renge kyō*.

293. Reeves, *The Lotus Sutra*, 347.

294. Nikkyō Niwano, *The Lotus Sutra: The Life and Soul of Buddhism*. (Tokyo: Kosei Publishing Co., 1970), 179–80.

295. Fuji-kō 富士講.

296. Butsu-ryū-kō 仏立講.

297. 長松清風.

298. 日扇.

299. Hokke-shū Happon-ha 法華宗八品派.

300. Hokke-shū Honmon-ryu 法華宗本門派.

301. *okagemairi* お蔭参り.

302. *eejanaika* ええじゃないか.

303. *nukemairi* 抜参り.

304. Soka Gakkai 創価学会 (originally Soka Kyōiku Gakkai 創価教育学会).

305. Risshō Kōsei-kai 立正佼成会 (up to 1960 Dai-Nippon Risshō Kōsei-kai 大日本立正交成会).

306. Reiyūkai 霊友会.

307. Girō Seno'o 妹尾義郎.

308. 本多日生.

309. Tōitsukaku 統一閣 Literally "Unity Palace."

310. Kenpon Hokke-shū 顕本法華宗.

311. Nichishō Honda, *Hokekyō Kōgi* 法華経講義 [Lectures on the Lotus Sutra] (Tōkyō: Hakubunkan, 1917).

312. 天晴会.

313. 自慶会.

314. 智法思国会.

315. *Risshō Daishi* 立正大師.

316. Dai Nippon Nichiren Shugi Seinen Dan 大日本日蓮主義青年団.

317. Shinkō Bukkyo Seinen Dōmei 新興仏教青年同盟.

318. *Kangyō Hachiman Shō* 諫暁八幡鈔 [Admonition with Hachiman].

319. *Shinri undō* 真理運動.

320. Tomomatsu Entei 友松円諦.

321. Ōmoto-kyō 大本教.

322. Kyōgyō shinshō 教行信証. Translated in: Yoshifumi Ueda, ed., *The True Teaching, Practice and Realization of the Pure Land Way: A Translation of Shinran's Kyōgyōshinshō*, vol. 4 (Kyoto: Hongwanji International Center, 1983–90).

323. Makiguchi Tsunesaburō 牧口常三郎.

324. Toda Jōsei 戸田城聖.

325. In Hirata's *Shinteki Nisshū Ron* 神敵二宗教論 [Two schools are enemies of the gods], an appendix to *Shutsujō Shōgo* 出定笑語.

326. Honmon-ryu (Happon-ha) 本門流 (八品派).

327. The ten realms referred to here are the realms of hells, hungry spirits, beasts (or animals), asuras, human beings, heavenly beings, śrāvakas, pratyekabuddhas, and buddhas.

328. The *"daimōku"* is the phrase *Namu myō hō renge kyō* 南無妙法蓮華教 ("Praise to the Wonderful Dharma Lotus Flower Sutra").

329. Nichiryū 日隆.

Bibliography

Anesaki, Masaharu. *Genshinbutsu to hosshinbutsu* 現身仏と法身仏 [The Historical Buddha and the Dharmakaya Buddha]. Tōkyō: Yūhōkan, 1901.

———, Konpon bukkyo 根本仏教 [Fundamental Buddhism]. Tōkyō: Hakubunkan, 1910.

Bodhi, Bhikkhu, trans. *The Connected Discourses of the Buddha: A Translation of the Saṃyutta Nikāya*. Boston: Wisdom Publications, 2000.

———, trans. *The Middle Length Discourses of the Buddha: A Translation of the Majjhima Nikāya*. Boston: Wisdom Publications, 1995.

Buddhist Text Translation Society, trans. *The Wonderful Dharma Lotus Flower Sutra, with Commentary by Tripitaka Master Hua*, 10 vols. San Francisco: Sino-American Buddhist Association, 1976–82.

van Buitenen, J. A. B., trans. *The Bhagavadagītā in the Mahābhārata: Text and Translation*. Chicago: University of Chicago Press, 1981.

Bunyiu, Nanjio. *Bonkan Taishō Shinyaku Hokekkyō* 梵漢對照新譯法華經 [A New Comparative Translation of the Lotus Sutra from Sanskrit and Chinese]. Kyoto: Jingenkai Shuppanbu, 1913.

Burnouf, Émile-Louis. *Le Lotus de la Bonne Loi*. 2 vols. Paris: Imprimerie Nationale, 1844 and 1852.

Conze, Edward, trans. *The Large Sutra on Perfect Wisdom*. Berkeley: University of California Press, 1975.

Donner, Neal, and Daniel B. Stevenson. *The Great Calming and Contemplation: A Study and Annotated Translation of the First Chapter of Chih-i's Mo-ho Chih-kuan*. Honolulu: University of Hawaii Press, 1993.

Groner, Paul. *Saicho: The Establishment of the Japanese Tendai School*. Berkeley: Asian Humanities Press, 1984.

Hakuin, Ekaku. *Hakuin-osho Zenshu* 白隠和尚全集 [The Collected Works of Hakuin]. 5 vols. Tōkyō: Ryugin-sha, 1934.Hattori, Ten'yū (Somon). *Sekirara* 赤裸々 [Nakedness]. Tōkyō: Tōhō Shoin, [between 1930 and 1931].

Hirata, Atsutane. *Shutsujō Shōgo* 出定笑語 [Laughter after Meditation]. [Japan, s.l.: s.n.], 1849.

Hubbard, Jamie, and Paul L. Swanson, eds. *Pruning the Bodhi Tree: The Storm over Critical Buddhism*. Honolulu: University of Hawaii Press, 1997.

Hurvitz, Leon, trans. *Scripture of the Lotus Blossom of the Fine Dharma (The Lotus Sūtra)*, rev ed. New York: Columbia University Press, 2009.

Iwamoto, Y., and Sakamoto Yukio. *Hokekyō* 法華経 3 vols. Tokyo: Iwanami Shoten, 1962, 1976, and 1989.

Katō, Bunnō, trans. *The Threefold Lotus Sutra: Innumerable Meanings, The Lotus Flower of the Wonderful Law, and Meditation on the Bodhisattva Universal Virtue.* Reviewed by W. E. Soothill and Wilhelm Schiffer. Kosei Publishing Company, Tokyo, 1971, 1975.

Kawaguchi, Ekai. *Bonzōdenyaku-myōhōbyaku-renge-kyō* 梵蔵伝訳妙法蓮華経 [A Translation from the Storehouse of Sanskrit Sutras: The Sutra of the White Flower of the Wonderful Dharma]. Tōkyō: Sekai Bunko Kankōkai, 1924.

Kawashima, Seishi. *A Glossary of Kumārajīva's Translation of the Lotus Sutra* 妙法法蓮華経訶典. Bibliotheca Philologica et Philosophica Buddica IV Tokyo: The International Research Institute for Advanced Buddhology, Soka University, 2001.

Kern, H., trans. *Saddharma-Puṇḍarīka: or, The Lotus of the True Law.* New York: Dover Publications, 1963.

Kim, Young-Ho. *Tao-sheng's Commentary on the Lotus Sūtra.* Albany: State University of New York Press, 1990.

Kubo, Tsugunari, and Yuyama, Akira, trans. *The Lotus Sutra: The White Lotus of the Marvelous Law.* Rev. ed. Tokyo and Berkeley: Bukkyō Dendō Kyōkai and Numata Center for Buddhist Translation and Research, 2007.

LaFleur, William R. *The Karma of Words: Buddhism and the Literary Arts in Medieval Japan.* Berkeley: University of California Press, 1983.

Liebenthal, Walter. *Chao Lun: The Treatises of Seng-chao.* Hong Kong: Hong Kong University Press, 1968.

McRae, John, trans. *The Vimalakīrti Sutra.* Berkeley: Numata Center for Buddhist Translation and Research, 2004.

Motoori, Norinaga. *Motoori Norinaga Zenshū* 本居宣長全集 [The Complete Works of Norinaga Motoori]. Tōkyō: Chikuma Shobō, 1968–93.

———, *Tamakatsuma* 玉勝間 [Treasury of Essays]. Tōkyō: Iwanami Shoten, 1934.

Murakami, Senjo. *Bukkyō Tōitsuron* 仏教統一論 [A Treatise on the Unification of Buddhism]. Tōkyō: Shoshishinsui, 2011.

Murano, Senchū, trans. *The Lotus Sutra: The Sutra of the Lotus Flower of the Wonderful Dharma.* Tokyo: Nichiren Shu Shimbun, 1991.

Nichiren. *The Major Writings of Nichiren Daishonin.* Rev. ed., 7 vols. Tokyo: Nichiren Shoshu International Center, 1979–.

Niwano, Nikkyō, *The Lotus Sutra: The Life and Soul of Buddhism.* Tokyo: Kosei Publishing Co., 1970.

———, *Buddhism for Today: A Modern Interpretation of the Threefold Lotus Sutra.* Tokyo: Kosei Publishing Co., 1979.

Ogiwara, Unrai, and Tsuchida Katsuya. *Saddharmapuṇḍarīka-sūtram: Romanized and Revised Text of the Bibliotheca Buddhica Publication by Consulting a Skt. Ms. and Tibetan and Chinese Translations.* Tokyo: Seigo-Kenkyūka, 1934-35.

Oka, Kyōsui. *Bonbun Wayaku Hokekkyō* 梵文和訳法華経 [Lotus Sutra: A Japanese Translation from the Sanskrit]. Ōsaka: Yagō Shoten, 1924.

Pye, Michael. *Skillful Means: A Concept in Mahayana Buddhism.* London: Gerald Duckworth & Co., 1978. 2nd ed., London: Routledge, 2003.

Reeves, Gene, trans. *The Lotus Sutra: A Contemporary Translation of a Buddhist Classic.* Boston: Wisdom Publications, 2008.

Sato, Hiroaki, trans. *A Future of Ice: Poems and Stories of a Japanese Buddhist.* San Francisco: North Point Press, 1989.

———, trans. *Miyazawa Kenji: Selections.* Berkeley: University of California Press, 2007.

———, trans. *Spring & Asura: Poems of Kenji Miyazawa.* Chicago: Chicago Review, 1973.

Siderits, Mark, and Katsura Shōryū. *Nāgārjuna's Middle Way: Mūlamadhyamakakārikā*. Boston: Wisdom Publications, 2013.

Stone, Jacqueline I. *Original Enlightenment and the Transformation of Medieval Japanese Buddhism*. Honolulu: University of Hawaii Press, 1999.

Swanson, Paul L. *Foundations of T'ien-T'ai Philosophy: The Flowering of the Two Truths Theory in Chinese Buddhism*. Berkeley: Asian Humanities Press, 1989.

Tamura, Yoshio. *Hokke-kyō: shinri, seimei, jissen* 法華経：真理・生命・実践 . Tokyo: Chūō Kōron Sha, 1969 and 1991.

———. *Hongaku Shisō Ron* 本覚思想論 [Essays on Original Enlightenment Thought] (Tokyo: Shunjūsha, 1990).

———. "Japanese Culture, and the Tendai Concept of Original Enlightenment," in *Japanese Journal of Religious Studies* 14, nos. 2–3 (1987), 203–10.

———. *Japanese Buddhism: A Cultural History* (Tokyo: Kosei Publishing Co., 2000).

Tominaga, Nakamoto. *Chūkai Shutsujō Kōgo* 注解出定後語 [Emerging from Meditation]. Tōkyō: Ōzorasha, 1996.

———, *Emerging from Meditation*, trans. by Michael Pye. London: Duckworth, 1990.

Tominaga, Nakamoto, and Hattori Ten'yū (Somon). *Gappon Shitsujō Kōgō Sekirara* 合本出定後語赤裸々 [*Emerging from Meditation* and *Nakedness* in One Volume]. Tokyo: Komei-sha, 1902.

Tsukamoto, Keishō. *Source Elements of the Lotus Sutra*. Tokyo: Kosei Publishing Co., 2007.

Ueda, Yoshifumi, ed. *The True Teaching, Practice and Realization of the Pure Land Way: A Translation of Shinran's Kyōgyōshinshō*, 4 vols. Kyoto: Hongwanji International Center, 1983–90.

Watson, Burton, trans. *The Lotus Sutra*. New York: Columbia University Press, 1993.

———, trans. *The Lotus Sutra and Its Opening and Closing Sutras*. Tokyo: Soka Gakkai, 2009.

———, trans. *The Vimalakirti Sutra*. New York: Columbia University Press, 1997.

Ziporyn, Brook. *Evil and/or/as The Good: Omnicentricism, Intersubjectivity, and Value Paradox in Tiantai Buddhist Thought*. Cambridge: Harvard University Asia Center, 2009.

Index

Page numbers followed by "q" indicate quotations.

and Christianity vs. Nipponism, 143

About the Authors

YOSHIRŌ TAMURA was born in 1921 and raised in a Christian family in the commercial city of Osaka, Japan. During his first year as a college student in 1943, he was drafted to serve in the Japanese army and was sent to various overseas locations. Following World War II he graduated from the prestigious University of Tokyo as a student of Buddhism and Indian philosophy. His first teaching position for over fifteen years was at Tōyō University, first as associate professor and later as full professor. In 1972 he moved to the University of Tokyo, where he became the world's leading expert on Tiantai/Tendai thought, especially so-called "original enlightenment thought," and on the Lotus Sutra. Retiring from the University of Tokyo in 1982, he moved to the Nichiren-shu related Rissho University, also in Tokyo. Tamura passed away in March of 1989.

He was the author of many books, chapters of books, and journal articles in Japanese. At least three of his books, the first a translation from Chinese, have been translated into English, including *The Sutra of Innumerable Meanings* (the first part of *The Threefold Lotus Sutra*) (Kosei & Weatherhill, 1975), *Art of the Lotus Sutra* (Kosei, 1987) and *Japanese Buddhism: A Cultural History* (Kosei, 2000).

 GENE REEVES has been studying, teaching, and writing in Japan for twenty-five years, primarily on Buddhism and interfaith relations. Now an international advisor at Rissho Kosei-kai, he is also professor emeritus at Meadville Lombard Theological School in Chicago and a founder of the International Buddhist Congregation in Tokyo, where he serves as special minister. He has also served as the international advisor to the Niwano Peace Foundation and as the coordinator of an annual international seminar on the Lotus Sutra.

As a Buddhist teacher active in interfaith conversations and organizations, he travels frequently to China, Singapore, Taiwan, America, and Europe to give talks at conferences, universities, and churches, mainly on the Lotus Sutra. He is the translator of *The Lotus Sutra: A Contemporary Translation of a Buddhist Classic*, editor of *A Buddhist Kaleidoscope: Essays on the Lotus Sutra*, and author of *Stories of the Lotus Sutra*.

About Wisdom Publications

WISDOM PUBLICATIONS is the leading publisher of contemporary and classic Buddhist books and practical works on mindfulness. Publishing books from all major Buddhist traditions, Wisdom is a nonprofit charitable organization dedicated to cultivating Buddhist voices the world over, advancing critical scholarship, and preserving and sharing Buddhist literary culture.

To learn more about us or to explore our other books, please visit our website at www.wisdompubs.org. You can subscribe to our eNewsletter, request a print catalog, and find out how you can help support Wisdom's mission either online or by writing to:

Wisdom Publications
199 Elm Street
Somerville, Massachusetts 02144 USA

You can also contact us at 617-776-7416, or info@wisdompubs.org.

Wisdom is a 501(c)(3) organization, and donations in support of our mission are tax deductible.

Wisdom Publications is affiliated with the Foundation for the Preservation of the Mahayana Tradition (FPMT).

Also Available from Wisdom Publications

The Lotus Sutra
A Contemporary Translation of a Buddhist Classic
Gene Reeves
504 pages, $19.95

"This translation is immediately the new standard."
—Taigen Dan Leighton

The Stories of the Lotus Sutra
Gene Reeves
Foreword by Rafe Martin
384 pages, $18.95

"A transforming read."—*Mandala*